21ST CENTURY FAITH

21ST CENTURY FAITH

RADICAL MISSION IN A NEW MILLENNIUM

Barry Linney

Marshall Pickering
An Imprint of HarperCollinsPublishers

Marshall Pickering is an imprint of
HarperCollins*Religious*
part of HarperCollins*Publishers*
77–85 Fulham Palace Road, London W6 8JB
www.christian-publishing.com

First published in Great Britain in 2000
by Marshall Pickering

1 3 5 7 9 10 8 6 4 2

Copyright © 2000 Barry J. Linney

Barry Linney asserts the moral right to be identified
as the author of this work.

A catalogue record for this book
is available from the British Library.

ISBN 0 551 03233 2

Printed and bound in Great Britain by
Caledonian International Book Manufacturing Ltd, Glasgow

To my Dad,
Henry Linney,

whose gleams of faith were sparks to my own.

CONTENTS

INTRODUCTION

Human History seems always to be without God. Yet God's will
and working run through everything. Ultimately His will is done.

Christopher Blumhardt

In these early days of the 21st Century much is being said in the
sacred and secular world about the 'spiritual expectation' that is
prevalent in people's lives. Such talk highlights the fact that the
old certainties of yesterday have disappeared, and people are
facing the future with distrust and bewilderment. We are told
that people are becoming much more spiritually aware and are
prepared to give spiritual answers to things and to seek spiritual
experiences, where even a few years ago this would not have
been the case. Clairvoyants are advertising in national newspapers to offer advice about how money can be best invested in
stocks and shares; wealthy, powerful executives are prepared to
arrange their office furniture in such a way so as to be aligned
more spiritually; many leading rock and movie stars are turning
to spiritual things and even writing about them in their songs;
films, TV shows, books, board-games and card-games take it for
granted that people are able to handle diverse spiritual and
supernatural thoughts. In the United States we see a massive
interest in Native Indian Spirituality, with people wanting to get

connected with creation in a natural and spiritual way. In the United Kingdom, following the sudden death of Princess Diana, we saw some clues that people are possibly searching for a communal identity and are wanting to come out of their isolated existence and to experience a sense of togetherness and belonging.

We are also presented with the fact that science itself, which offered so much hope to people a hundred or so years ago, has failed to deliver what it promised and has left people disillusioned and looking again to dimensions other than science to provide a sense of purpose and hope.

None of these things is disputed in this book. Indeed, this book in many ways seeks to build on much of this. The reality for the Church, though, is that for most people on our high streets none of these so-called spiritual developments is impacting them in a way that causes them to think any more seriously about attending church, what churches are there for, or starting a relationship with Jesus as we would present this to them.

However we may interpret this spiritual awareness, evangelism as we are currently doing it is not working. We only have to look back over the 'Decade of Evangelism' (i.e. the 1990s) to see that there has been very little evangelistic fruit, and that our society and the Church to which we continue to owe our allegiance are still poles apart in their thinking and relating. Whatever may be happening in people 'out there', the Church does need to change 'within itself' if it is to be a voice in the belief-patterns of people in the 21st Century.

It is out of this challenge that the mission of the Church seeks to find its fullest expression. The call to share our faith in Jesus Christ, the true Saviour and safety of our world, to share the good news of the Kingdom, is still as alive and as opportune as ever it has been. To seize the day remains a live and challenging opportunity for us. It means that we will need go to the core of our beliefs and ask afresh what it means to be a Christian in today's world, and how we can best influence our society for God.

This is not another book about how the Church can update its methodology – the old dressed up in the new, as it were; it is about discovering a new way of being, a new identity out of which the Church can launch its evangelistic challenge. Many churches are wanting to update their ministry in an attempt to become relevant again and to integrate with society. Yet making the message relevant by simply dressing it up in some new and trendy clothes is really not much more than trying to teach an old dog new tricks. This is not what this book is about. This book is about re-thinking the way we see the world and the nature and shape of evangelism within the world of which we are inescapably a part. It asks what evangelism and the evangelical Church will look like in the 21st Century if we are to attempt to put the Church on people's agenda again.

World-view

I was in a church recently where the speaker was talking about being in the world but not of it. This brought back many memories to me, because it was the sort of sermon that I had myself preached many times in the past. In fact even one of the quotes was a favourite of mine – J. B. Phillips' translation of Romans 12:2, 'Do not let the world squeeze you into its mould.' I am not fully sure what may have happened to me in the intervening years, but this time round I felt that the sermon had a fairly high 'cringe factor'. It made me empathize a little more with all those people who used to have to listen to me each week!

What made this sermon so noticeable was that the world was being seen in an almost totally negative way. 'Not being squeezed into its likeness' showed the world to be bad and something that needed to be constantly resisted and opposed. I know where the preacher was coming from, because I used to approach things in the same way. It is almost as if I enjoyed seeing the world and developments in it through negative eyes – at times, I dare say, even scare-tactic eyes.

But rather than thinking of the world as 'worldly' and negative, perhaps a 21st Century view of evangelism will mean that we start to see the world in a much more positive light. It is one thing to see the world as essentially bad with occasional glimpses of good, and quite another to see the world as good with areas of bad that need to be discerned as such. This negative view of the world is often extended to the people in it. Things are 'of the world' and people are 'worldly', which means that anything with this label is seen in a less-than-positive way. This ranges from the commercial and secular nature of Christmas to the fun that most children have at Halloween. Yet if we are to engage those outside the Church, seeing 'the world' and 'their world' in negative terms means that our approach is going to be uphill all the way, because we believe that we have so much to both undo and re-do. Yet if we were to see through more positive eyes, it would mean that we would approach the world believing that Christ is already abundantly at work in it and has already made considerable progress. It is God's world and he has not resigned as its creator, sustainer and redeemer. If we are more influenced by the negative aspects of the world rather than its positive ones, then it seems that we are giving a greater place to the enemy of God than we are giving to God himself. A worldless God easily paves the way for a Godless world. To give more credit to the absence of God than to the presence of God in his world is a step towards becoming a Church with an anaemic view of God the Almighty.

Hallo-ian

When I was a pastor on the south coast of England I lived in a block of flats with an intercom buzzer to let people in. It was Halloween and, as is the custom at this time of year, I was visited by young people 'tricking or treating'. As the buzzer would go I would either answer it or go down and tell them in a gentle but firm way that the Lord Jesus was not pleased about what they were doing. The non-plussed response that I got ranged from 'You what?' to 'Yeah, right' and left me feeling firstly, that I had simply failed to communicate to them, but more importantly, that I was sowing truth that would work against this potentially harmful and damaging aspect of their young lives.

This last Halloween things were very different. When the trick or treaters arrived, I opened the door and mostly replied that I would give them a treat. This usually meant me giving them some chocolate bars or crisps. On one rather humorous occasion I said 'treat' and still got sprayed with that liquid foam stuff, and subsequently I heard their dad's voice round the corner sternly telling them that they should not have done that, as I had said 'treat'! Well, anyway, the point is that a change had taken place in the way I saw the world, and a change, little did I know, that was to work for the good.

A few days later some neighbours invited me up for a fireworks party where some of the children and young people in the same street would be present. And, lo and behold, some of the children who had called on me for Halloween were there, and remembered me. They also got to know in the course of the evening that I was a 'vicar' (as they put it), and also got to know me a little more as a friendly neighbour. There now exists a relationship between these young people and me, and it was only afterwards that I realized that they now see me, a Christian leader, as someone who is kind and generous (at least with crisps and sweets!) rather than someone who is grumpy and judgemental about something which they think of as harmless fun and which almost everyone their age does. One of the lads, called Ian, started attending a church-run youth club as a result of getting to know some of the local Christians.

Of course, I am not saying that everything about Halloween is good – in the more extreme cases there can be involvement with the occult – but for most children and young people the reality is that it is just fun. It demonstrates to me that when we take the sting out of the way we see the world we are in a much better position to build relationships, and we are able to identify with the day-to-day realities of people's lives.

Aliens too!

Some evangelistic seminars seem to portray the world as 'alien territory' and Christians as snipers carefully checking what is out there in order to plan the best invasion. The mission of the Christian is being done in hostile territory; it is a case of 'us and them', and only the best strategy will enable us to win. However, to embark upon an evangelistic endeavour with such a view of the world is hardly helpful to its success. To perceive the Church as being so separate from the rest of humanity belies our call to be both cultural as well as counter-cultural, which can only effectively happen if the Christian community exists as a pure and simple part of the human community.

On one of the training programmes for young people that I used to run something that one of the church leaders wrote brought home to me the reality of just how hard we need to work to get a balanced view of things. We used to ask for references from the church leaders, asking them to list the strengths and weaknesses of the candidate. On the application form for one of the young people, under the section where it asked for 'Strengths', the referee had put things like 'Good sense of humour, likeable, hard-working', but in the 'Weaknesses' column he had put 'When with unbelievers tends to mingle.'

The evangelical mind-set has frequently been one that maintains that we need to stand apart from the world, because the world is contaminated with sin and evil, and if we show too much identity with and interest in the world, then we too could become infected by it.

Such an approach does need to be challenged, for the sake of those we are called to share our lives with. We only have to think about the Christmas story to see that the way of salvation is the way of identification and involvement. The incarnation is God's 'OK' to humanness and the world. It is OK to be involved in the world. This is the way of salvation – there really is no other way. If our beliefs prevent us from rendering service to the world, because a 'thought gap' exists between the way the world sees itself and the way we see it, we are not really doing justice to this notion of involvement at personal cost. A radical re-think is required.

Who said 'It's a beautiful world'?

A preferred interpretation of Romans 12:2 is that we should not become wholly immersed in the world because of its tendency to corrupt, rather than that we should not be open to its good. Society and the people who make it up are bitter/sweet, capable of tremendous good and also immense harm. A world-view that affirms the intrinsic goodness of creation can be tested to its limits, since we only have to scratch the surface to find a malevolent evil in many situations. There are many things in society that we rightfully scorn and oppose – things that devalue and abuse people or elevate them to God-like status. Yet this should not blind us to the fact that society has both veins running through it – the good and the bad. The problem is not that the world is as bad as it is; the miracle is that the world is as *good* as it is. The One who called it 'good' is still doing so, and he will watch over it to see that it can finally be confirmed as 'very good' (Genesis 1:2, 17, 25; cf. 1:31). Goodness is woven into our world and will ultimately win; it is ever present to be redeemed and fanned into flame.

What is for certain, though, is that whatever may be the 'lot' of this world, we, the Church, are part of it and must take our place within it and alongside it. Whilst we will undoubtedly struggle to make sense of this bitter/sweet symphony, the challenge to the Church should not be one of disassociation by creating an alternative world that is a reaction against this one, but rather one of active association and costly identification. Such involvement will require discernment to identify where society and the values of those who make it up are going wrong and need a corrective voice.

So what follows in this book is written with a passion for the success of evangelical Christianity. It is a vision for the Church, a desire to see it win in the 21st Century. It is born out of a desire to see people and society in touch with the Christian faith, and yet it seeks to address some of those areas of the evangelical mindset that hinder this most important of tasks. It is written with the conviction that things in the evangelical Church need to change. It also acknowledges, though, that the Church itself is on a pilgrimage and, whatever may be the respective positions of the bushel and the light at this particular moment in history, the One who creates both light and dark is ever at work in his Church to ensure that it remains a beacon of light to a world that is constantly in need of the light of its Creator.

Chapter 1

MASK

You had shot my heart through with the arrows of your love, and I carried your words thrust deep into my inner being.

Augustine

In the talks I have given about evangelism I have often told the story of the time when I was speaking at a church meeting in a town I had never visited before. All my attempts at arriving early and unruffled had slowly evaporated as I got more and more lost driving around in the dark, trying to find the church building. After stopping the car several times and trying to find where I was on the numerous maps and directions I had been given, I wound down the window and asked a local. Eventually, after giving the matter some considerable thought, he rubbed his chin and quite seriously said to me, 'You know, you can't get to there from here.' Of course, looking back now, it's funny, but at the time it was almost the end! I was *here*, I had to get to *there*, and I was very, very late.

I sometimes think that we Christians make the same mistake that this local man made. We say to people on their own life's journey, 'You can't get to Jesus from here. You have to start from somewhere else.' But this is just as impossible for them as it was for me. They have no other starting-place, for, good or bad, this is where they are, and if they are to move forward at all, they have to start from where they are.

If we are to meaningfully face the evangelistic challenge, then we need to be bridge-builders in today's society, and we need to build bridges with all kinds of people who often face a multitude of different issues. No matter where people are, we absolutely must start where they are at and not where we would like them to be.

As these multitudinous issues are explored in the chapters that follow, it could appear that our own Christian identity is being defaced, that we are moving beyond recognized boundaries. But this is not the case at all. In fact, it is imperative that we have a secure grasp of our own identity as Christians if we are to embrace an evangelism that will work in a New Millennium. Bridge-building will only work if the bridgehead is deeply rooted in the historic faith of the Church, and if our personal relationship with God is dynamic and alive, and if the arrows of his love do indeed sink deep into our inner being. Bridges that span rivers, ravines and roads require firm footings. That which is not rooted is soon uprooted. This means that our inner certainty about who we are as Christians and about what we belong to needs to be sure and steadfast. It is not that we become like Jim Carrey in the film *The Mask*, where he is so unsure about his own identity that he becomes different people according to the need of the moment. Such assurance and identity comes out of a deep personal walk with God, as well as from our own place within the evangelical community and our association with its own ethos and life.

Most issues of identity are hard fought and hard won, but when these issues have been faced it is time to move on, in the certainty of this victory, to embrace a changing world with new-found strength and conviction. Yet for evangelism to work and for the Church to gain a higher national and social profile, we need to be able to move beyond simply affirming our own identity. This is something that we seem to have been blissfully unaware of.

Ears please!

I thought I'd take Peter to the 'Seeker Service'. Lots of churches were doing them and they seemed to hold so much promise. The evening was entitled 'You're Born, You Live, You Die – End of Story?' I thought this was not a particularly good starting-place, but perhaps things would get better. The first half hour included a reading from the book of Revelation, a hymn and a prayer. Then came a drama and some songs which were all focused on the need for a person's life to be changed by an encounter with Jesus. The talk, based on the title of the evening, suggested that we need to give abundant thought to what happens when we die. Yet these things were not particularly live issues for Peter. If he did believe in life after death, he certainly didn't see himself as living in the eternal flames of hell. The evening ended by putting a rather negative slant on Peter's life, suggesting that unless he responded to the Christian message, his life would not count for much.

Such 'Seeker Services' are a good example of the Church trying to be relevant but succeeding in being relevant only to itself. We all tried such services – I certainly did – but rather than listening to those outside, we were still only speaking to them after listening to our own heartbeat.

'Seeker Services' did not work because we failed to realize that, while the Church is very good at preaching, it is not quite so good at listening. If the evangelistic challenge means seeing things from the perspective of those we are attempting to reach, then this will involve entering into their concerns and values, being prepared to pass on things that are part of our identity, and allowing their views, no matter how outlandish, to stand as part of their identity. Rather than breezing in with our agenda of conversion, we should let this person's own life speak first. They have authentic human stories to tell, and their response to God may take forms that we simply do not see.

It is right that we, the evangelical Church, having won things for ourselves, should make these things serve a higher purpose.

For example, when the historicity and therefore the reliability and authority of the Bible was under severe question, it was right at the time for the Church to defend the Bible and affirm its historical reliability. But now that we have done that and this concern is not the one of the moment, many of the issues of authority and reliability that fill many sermons, books and seminars become redundant. We need to move on to the application of biblical truth in the fast-changing world of today. Similarly, earlier this century some sections of the Church were so busy defending their own apostolic veracity that they partly forgot why such things were important in the first place. They are important because they speak of the historic foundation of the Church through those commissioned by Christ himself, who called his newly constituted community to go out to others and speak of him. All too often we can be so caught up with defending our own credentials and addressing our own concerns that we forget that there is a world outside that breathes in the same air as we do but breathes out a very different set of priorities. The evangelistic challenge will attempt to address some of this disparity.

'In this ever-changing world in which we live'

The shape, colour and profile of much of the evangelical Church has been influenced by developments in the wider world, and it is right that we should constantly reassess our own values and beliefs in the light of the world in which we are called to shine as lights. We do not need to fight yesterday's battles, however, nor do we need to cling tenaciously to things that are now rightfully ours; instead we should be reaching out to take hold of future questions. What was food for yesterday is stale manna for today. We need to respond to new and fresh challenges with the vigour that is ours through the treasures that those who have gone before us have handed on to us.

Through the looking-glass

Something that illustrated to me the need for a greater empathy between the Church and the world was a discussion group I took part in at a one-day seminar run by a missionary-based organization. Those attending the seminar were divided up into buzz groups and were asked to discuss the negotiables and the non-negotiables of a church. When the feedback from each group was given, the answers were mostly to do with our own concerns – preaching the gospel as Jesus did, baptism, communion, tithing, prayer, Bible study, worship. Whilst these things are valuable to us and are an important part of our identity, we will start seeing them in a different light when our own heart beats for the people who remain outside our walls. If we understand such activities as ways of affirming our own identity so that we are better resourced to meet the needs of those who know nothing of these activities, then the only non-negotiable we would have suggested would have been a way of 'doing church' that has at its core a deep and pervading concern for those who do not yet belong. The non-negotiables of a church from this perspective would probably have had more to do with sharing the life and love of Jesus in the practical realities of life, and with being a community that is part of the local community but reflects the love of Christ into its difficulties and hurts. More of this later.

To see things through the eyes of those outside means that our language, our concerns and our very heartbeat become the things that help us to reach the world whilst remaining part of it. It means that whilst we may value things within the Church – such as charismatic gifting, the place of music and worship, being part of a cell group, good Bible teaching, developments in media technology that enhance a sense of divine encounter – we recognize that all these things exist for the Church, whereas the Church is meant to exist for society. They are not what the Church is about; they simply help the Church to be what it is about.

At the main Sunday morning service of a certain church I once spoke about the need to be open to new ways of doing things that break with the Church tradition of the past. After the service one dear old man came up to me and said that he agreed that we need to change, since much of what we do as Christians is very selfish. Our services are geared to believers and would make the unbeliever feel totally lost. Then he said that some things must never change, though, like the Ten Commandments. He said 'Thou shalt keep the Sabbath' means that it is wrong for people to work or buy things or watch TV on a Sunday. This man recognized the need to change, but to suggest that the Sabbath law puts in the wrong the countless millions who shop and go to work on Sundays is to see things in a way that most people certainly do not.

This is an isolated example, and many Christians themselves would not see Sundays in these terms. But the point remains that we are all prepared to change except in those areas that help to define us, whatever they may be. As soon as we start to touch things that appear to threaten our own Christian identity, we recoil.

Changes in the way we think have been an historic part of the Church's own life. They have often come about as a result of events or crises that have shed new light on the way we see and apprehend, on the way we think and act. This in turn has led to a new understanding and the recognition that there now exists another way of seeing what we are looking at – rather like two artists' impressions drawn from different angles. For example, after the Holocaust many theologians started to think in new ways about how God related to his world, with the result that in some circles God was seen as much more personal and involved in the world – humanity's suffering was God's suffering. He is not just a majestic Lord up in heaven, away from all the suffering of humanity; he is the crucified God, he suffers when his children suffer.

Other events in the world have meant seeing the Christian faith through the eyes of the poor, the dispossessed and the powerless. What does the Christian faith affirm when seen from their position? This does give a very different picture from the perspective of those with wealth and power, and it affects the way we see a number of issues.

There is also the ecological challenge. Interpreting the Bible from this perspective makes very different reading from the perspective in which the Earth is seen as something that is at the disposal of humans, with little thought about the consequences of our abuse of the environment.

An evangelistic agenda that starts to think about things from the perspective of those outside the Church asks not 'How can we get our message across?' but 'What are they open to receive?'; not 'How can we get them to see things our way?' but 'How do they look at things?'; not 'How can we convince them of the need for salvation?' but 'What is salvation to them?'

Let's go fly a kite

I like the idea that a kite can only fly when it is connected to the ground. The higher it goes, the stronger that which links it to the ground needs to be. If we cut its connection, it just comes tumbling down. The only reason it can fly at all is because it is attached to the ground. As issues in this book are explored, the kite will fly pretty high at times, for in trying to see things from the perspective of those outside the Church, we will be forced to ask some very searching questions, tested to the limits of what we think is 'Christian' and compelled to rethink some of the values that help to define us. These areas of identity will be looked at in the chapters that follow, and it is precisely in our response to the issues raised that we will find out how rooted we are in our own identity, and yet also how prepared we are to meet the challenges of the world we inhabit. What giddy heights must we soar to if we are to connect with them, and at the same time remain connected to the root and basis of our faith?

It is in this area of inner certainty and of authentic relationship with God that the evangelistic challenge will expose our own weaknesses. Many of us today can all too frequently live in a kind of inner apartheid – we segregate out a small corner of pious activities, and then can make no sense of the rest of our lives, or indeed of how our beliefs intersect with the lives of those with whom we rub shoulders every day. Dealing with our doubts, fears and uncertainties is central to the challenge.

Alongside this, it also needs to be acknowledged that there is much in people's world-view that is destructive to their own and others' well-being. In kite flying we do not simply let go of who we are and affirm those things that we believe to be damaging; rather, we actively engage with the whole of the person we are meeting. We need to avoid the extreme that debunks the mission of the Church as irrelevant or sees it as something that is so passive as to be almost of no effect. The Church has to have an identity that is distinct from the world, or else we shall cease to be able to minister to it.

Such evangelistic identity impinges on *being* as well as *doing*. To be self-aware and self-assured is to be enabled to empower the outsider without losing ourselves. To be convinced that we own that which really does have within it the power of eternity means that it is no longer an argument between us and them, it is no longer me needing others to agree with me to affirm me and the rightness of my beliefs; rather, it is a matter of existing in such a way that others may become more than they are. It is very much like something that Nelson Mandela said in his inaugural speech:

Our deepest fear is not that we are inadequate. Our deepest fear is that we are powerful beyond measure. It is our light, not our darkness, that most frightens us. We ask ourselves, Who am I to be brilliant, gorgeous, talented and fabulous? Actually, who are we not to be? Your playing small doesn't serve the world. There's nothing enlightened about shrinking so that other people won't feel insecure around you. As we let our light shine, we unconsciously give other people permission to do the same. As we are liberated from our own fear, our presence automatically liberates others.

Such assurance never sides with corruption but transforms it. The reader will be asked to think about these things in later chapters.

Well, well, well!

Mary came into a relationship with the Lord through the ministry of my church. She was fresh from the world; she came to us through relationships that she had with Christians, but apart from this she had had little contact with the church. About six months after she started to occasionally attend church, I left to run a Christian training programme, but I met her again about two years later. She defensively told me that she didn't go to church much now because she worked in a betting shop and others in the church were giving her grief about it, saying that she had been a Christian for over two years now, and it was no longer appropriate for her to have such a job.

Mikey and Catriona had been converts for about a year when they were gently told by the church that, as they had been Christians for some time and were still cohabiting, they should perhaps start to think and plan towards getting married in the next six months or so.

These are not isolated incidents, for I have met dozens of Marys, Mikeys and Catrionas over the years, and the issues most important to them have not been about the moral dilemmas of working in a betting shop, co-habiting, smoking, swearing, drinking too much, playing the National Lottery, reading horoscopes or watching '18'-rated movies. These are undoubtedly things about which many Christians feel strongly, but which are of little consequence to those from outside the Church.

A real and personal meeting with the risen Christ will undoubtedly mean change. If someone's life remains largely dry and barren in what is meant to be a growing, loving relationship, then the authenticity of such a faith can seem spurious. However, people change in relationships as the relationship itself changes and grows. The Church is right to expect change, but it should expect a change that comes from a growing faith and a more loving and personal relationship, rather than wanting the change to define the nature of the relationship. Here our task is to provide an environment where such faith can grow.

Jesus' encounter with the woman at the well has something to teach us here. Her life was not what it should have been by the standards of the day (and even by our standards today!), and yet Jesus was able to build a relationship with her which was non-threatening but which had sufficient impact on her life to cause her to tell the whole village about him.

The story tells us what is important, and yet it does not tell us that Jesus condemned her cohabitation or her lifestyle (even though many sermons I have heard have implied this), only that he recognized the deeper issues which were at work in her life and into which he could build his own identity. He did not tell her that she was wrong to live like this; he met her where she was at. He knew that if she could truly find herself in him, then these other aspects of her life, that helped to give her some identity as a person, would be dealt with. The story tells of someone who was thirsting for something more in life (John 4:13–14). Jesus knew this and said that only by being in relationship with him, the source of all living water, could her thirst really be quenched.

As in my opening story in this chapter, he was not saying, 'You can't get there from here.' He was recognizing where she was and saying, 'You can get anywhere from here.' The account of the woman's activity in her village shows us that this encounter with Jesus was transformational, and in time her lifestyle changed as a result of this. It is in genuine encounter with Christ that people are changed into his likeness. However, the relationship must come before the rules, and it is out of this dynamic that change should be expected. Our task in situations like this is to discern the authenticity of the relationship itself and to help this to grow, rather than imposing rules that will crush the relationship.

A smouldering wick

This was well illustrated to me at a lunchtime workplace meeting for people who were outside the Church but who were interested in Christianity. While I gave my talk one woman in particular listened attentively, showing amazement, bewilderment and even dismay at some of the things I said, but she did not venture to say anything in the discussion that followed. Afterwards I approached her to ask if she had enjoyed the meeting. She told me that she had and, in the long talk that followed, I was once again surprised and humbled by the truth that every face tells a story. She told me where she was at in her own spiritual journey. She believed in God, but had not come to the sort of decision of faith that she felt was being asked of her by her friends. Nor was she ready to disavow some of her other beliefs. For example, she believed that all religions worshipped the same God but in different ways; that good works alone were enough to make us all right; that everyone would be united in a blissful afterlife. Also, she did not think that going to church was necessary, as she could commune with God when she was walking in the country, thinking about the way he had made the trees and the flowers and so on. These are the kind of beliefs that evangelism is often concerned about, since they detract from the decisiveness of conversion and commitment to Christ.

Whilst I did not agree with her in an unqualified sense, when she asked for my opinion, I did not tell her she was wrong. Her late husband had not been a churchgoer and had not expressed much of a faith in God, but had been a good man. When she asked me what I thought about her meeting up with him in eternity, I said that I could not answer for something which is God's decision alone, but I also affirmed her belief that God is good and loving and that her husband was in his hands. She told me that when she had asked another clergyman about this he had told her that her husband was probably not going to be in heaven, since he did not believe.

Some may feel that it was wrong to affirm something that I should have 'passed' on. But we must take seriously Jesus' words that it is not the mission of the Son of God to even put out a smouldering wick. To me her smouldering wick of faith was the most important thing here. To dampen it by telling her that she was wrong to believe these things or that I could not comment on these matters would have been to discourage her. I was more concerned about trying to fan into life a smouldering wick of hope and faith than I was about preserving some kind of dogmatism that is in itself beyond the scope of human reason anyway. The greater need is that of genuine and authentic identification with the concerns of those with whom we seek to build relationships and to share the good news of God, and where this involves no significant compromise of our beliefs, I suggest that we need to be prepared to be flexible.

When she had finished talking to me her face was radiant. I had spent half an hour listening to her life experiences – her losses, her suffering in East Germany – and so I was not just agreeing in a vacuum but had listened carefully to the concerns she felt. I thought that what she needed was to have the faith that she did possess encouraged rather than discouraged. The latter had already happened to her when she had talked to other people and, indeed, was one of the reasons why she did not attend church. But I believe that if the Christians whom she knew were to handle their relationship with her in a more positive way, her faith would grow and blossom.

When we are secure in our own beliefs and attitudes it gives us the stability that we need to identify with other people's search for spiritual identity. Often we build walls to protect ourselves, because we are uncertain about our faith, or because our faith is really a faith in man-made religious systems rather than a faith in God himself. When we have clearly put our roots down into God we are then able to embrace that which is stormy and tempestuous, without fear of being uprooted. As we face the issues that confront people in their spiritual pilgrimage, our own rootedness will mean that relationships can be built with openness and honesty. As we sink our foundations deep down into God and into those things that he has given his Church, the relationship that we have with him can become more dynamic and personal and less stilted by religious systems that choke creativity and spontaneity. To the hungry this will mean being filled with a more unshakeable confidence to cope with the complexities of life and faith.

The mask which not only hid our real identity but also provided a superficial face for each occasion can be put away when we have learned to be ourselves. This finding ourselves is ultimately done as we learn to face the other with openness, whilst constantly celebrating the glory of the Christian tradition. The capacity to be rooted in our own identity whilst openly engaging with others is not only essential to the evangelistic challenge; it is the very soil out of which such substance grows.

To think through some of these risks and identity issues, read on.

Chapter 2

EVANG'U'LISM ... U WHAT?!

Every attempt to impose the gospel by force, to run after people and proselytize them, to use our own resources to arrange the salvation of other people, is both futile and dangerous.

Dietrich Bonhoeffer

Everything was well prepared for the 'seeker-friendly service'. We all knew our roles, we had rehearsed them together the required number of times, and the prayer before the service felt good and positive, and we all believed that God was going to move in a special way. As we saw the guests start to come in, we could see a number of faces that we did not know, and so we knew that we had succeeded in getting in a number of non-Christians. As I walked among the congregation before we were due to start, Doreen, one of our best-loved members, came up to me and said, 'I've been praying for Ted [her husband] to come to church for so many years, and tonight is the answer to my prayers. I know the Lord is at work! Make sure you really give it your best tonight in your preaching. I am really believing that the Lord will touch him.'

Well, I did sock it to Ted, and to the rest of them, and it felt good! I felt sure that God was going to open Ted's heart and mind in new ways. I even had a lot of compliments afterwards about how anointed the message was, and, even if I say so myself, it was. God had really given me a timely message for many people in that place on that particular occasion.

The only problem was that Ted didn't become a Christian, and did not start going to church.

Neither did Sue, or Paul, or Nigel, or Kevin, or Anna, or Helen. The list could go on and on – all people whom we thought would be 'zapped' by hearing a verbal message by a preacher who was intent on seeing them come to faith. It could equally have been by hearing some amazing testimony, or reading a tract, or watching a video, or seeing something unusual happen – something that we hoped and believed would be that special touch by God that would make them change their entire belief system and lifestyle.

Over the years I have met scores of Doreens and Teds, and invariably the story ends in the same way.

And it is not just stories I could tell. I have been to many places in Britain, America and Europe and seen the same situation. We evangelicals, in our rightful zeal for God, are driven to convert people, and in so doing we often fail to win the people whom we thought we would win, and sometimes we even discourage them from continuing their spiritual exploration.

One of the reasons for such evangelistic failures is that one way or another, evangelism is thought of as getting people to join us on our quite distinctive terms – people are either 'in' or 'out'. The gospel will sort them out – the sheep from the goats, the chaff from the wheat. Their response to the gospel message is all we need to know in order to be able to categorize them. The hard reality for us to face, though, is that most people in the Western world find someone telling them the gospel or trying to 'win them for Christ' a big turn-off. We may kid ourselves with some anecdotal conversion stories from a 'seeker service' that was supposed to be a user-friendly and accessible introduction to Christianity, but such success stories are the exception rather than the rule. Our evangelism isn't working, and unless we change the way we approach it, we will continue to lose credibility with more and more people and we will become a minority sect in a world that has left us behind.

Whilst this whole book is about evangelism, other chapters deal with evangelism through some wider issues, since what we do evangelistically comes out of what we are and how we think. This chapter, however, is specifically about evangelistic practices as they are now. As we explore this issue we will look at some of the things that are not working as well as we would like them to, and we will also think about a future direction for evangelism. The rest of the book will attempt to show that evangelism has got to be done on a much broader base.

Our drive to convert

One of the results of the Enlightenment was an emphasis on progress. People were overjoyed by the prospects and possibilities that now seemed to be open to them. The idea of traversing the earth and discovering new territories was a dream that humankind eagerly pursued. This notion was in turn assimilated into the Christian scene. The progress of Christianity would ensure the Christianization of the whole world. Mission was understood by some as a quasi-military campaign to convert the heathen. The Christian mission was thought of as a companion movement to the Western imperialist outreach that was a result of the Enlightenment's expansionist view of the world. Christianity, it was thought, was an irresistible power that would shape the world. The broadening of our horizons and the means of now getting to these places meant that the faith could now triumph globally. Also, technical advances in printing meant that Christian literature was now much more widely available. Through the building of libraries and schools, the world could now be filled with the knowledge of the glory of the Lord.

So mission became identified with imperialism. Evangelists included in their understanding of mission the language of expansion, conquest and subjugation. Missionaries saw their spiritual work among the natives as coupled with the governmental rule of the country they were from. A good missionary took both God and government to the peoples. The British missionary was not only extending the Kingdom of God; he was extending the British Empire as well. The spread of Christianity went alongside the growth of commerce and the expansion of Western civilization.

In many ways this thinking has permeated our views of evangelism to the present day. We still use the language of war, imperialism and subjugation. 'Religious imperialism' is a sort of triumphalism in which we impose our belief systems on people so as to win them over to our way of thinking. Evangelism is seen as something that the powerful do to the less powerful; we who have the truth must impose what we have on others who do not have it.

Our concerted and often audacious efforts consist of working on people, but we justify this because it is for their own good and for the extension of the rule of God's Kingdom. This also affects the relationships that we have with those who are near and dear to us: wives work on their husbands and parents work on their children in an attempt to get them to see things their way. In the workplace many Christians make calculated attempts to 'witness', expecting that this will be the dawning of a new age for their colleagues, without really giving place to their hearers' own life-story or values.

The drive to convert is powerful. It defines our attitudes and actions towards people. It even affects the way we pray. Our prayers can be prayed with the purpose of moving people out of the darkness and into the light; we ask the Lord to 'bring them in'. Other religions serve another god, and this blindness needs to be removed with help from our prayers. People who reject our message are said to be 'hard-hearted' and need to be softened up by our supplications.

Witnessing is exalted to a position all on its own, almost as if the outcome is less significant than having done what we know we are supposed to do. All that matters is that we get the message across – and you never know, they might respond! The drive to share the gospel underlies much of the creative thinking being propounded by contemporary evangelists. A leading evangelical magazine recently included an article that suggested that we should start to use mainstream films, which in themselves are a popular pastime for people, so that we can do 'level-ground evangelism'. The idea is that we can watch the film together and hope that the conversation naturally leads to an exchange of views on the subject-matter, which in turn may lead to an opportunity to witness to them. The film will need to be chosen carefully, therefore, but there are plenty out there which raise issues of a moral, social and spiritual nature. Alternatively, we can give away free Christian videos for people to watch, and then get them to complete a questionnaire with an evangelistic angle.

It is certainly true that many contemporary films do raise issues of a spiritual and moral nature. This is an exciting and interesting phenomenon that we should certainly be prepared to engage with. I well remember the response of some friends of mine who watched the movie *Alive*, the story of a sports team whose aeroplane crash-landed in snowy, mountain wastelands. There they encountered the awe, wonder and mystery of God as they struggled to survive – eventually managing to do so only by eating the flesh of those who had been killed in the crash. They achieved the impossible by doing the unthinkable. Yet this story, which portrays the triumph of the human spirit, moral dilemma, fear and wonder amidst the majestic mountains, and a profound sense of God helping the survivors to pull through, made a deep impression on my friends.

Yet we must be careful not to push people too far and too narrowly in discussing a movie that raises moral and spiritual issues, which we may feel naturally lead on to evangelism. A sense of awe, marvel and mystery can in itself be a legitimate encounter with the God who himself remains mysterious and unfathomable in his eternal ways (Ecclesiastes 3:11). People's own experience of such things can be their unique and personal route to a greater appreciation of the things of God. Trying to impose a tight agenda may nip in the bud something which, given the right amount of time, could become a growing sense of God and of personal faith.

The motivation behind such an evangelistic attitude is indeed commendable, and the fire and zeal to see people come to a stronger faith in Christ is a distinctive that we evangelicals should never lose. But when it leads to such a drivenness and becomes such a defining part of the relationships that we build, it has to be questioned.

Recently I went through some brochures and books on what evangelism is. Below is a summary of the kind of language and imagery used in these publications:

Model	Church is seen as	Unbeliever is seen as	Christian needs to
Army	Marching against the enemy	Captive	Defeat
Lifeguard	Saving from disaster	Victim	Save
Storehouse	Resource	Impoverished/ starving	Supply/feed
Hospital	Curing the suffering	Sick	Cure
Judgement	Reform institute	Villain	Reform
Kingdom rule	Political kingdom	Pagan savage	Educate and civilize

All these pictures of the Church are in themselves biblical and convey something of what we are about, and so they remain important truths in the Church's self-understanding. However, when these pictures become tied to imperialistic attitudes, they can cause us to become triumphalistic and patronizing in our methods.

An example of this is the well-known description of evangelism as 'one beggar telling another beggar where to get food'. Such an approach fits well with the 'Lifeguard' and 'Storehouse' models and rightly adds a note of humility to our sharing of the gospel. But it can also convey a superior attitude in which we see ourselves as imparting our benefits to others through the spoken word. As long as evangelism is done using models such as the ones above, it is highly unlikely that Christians will see non-Christians as equals. As long as the picture is one in which the Church is seen as coming to an inadequate situation and providing the answers to it, we will only ever see evangelism from the vantage-point of the dominant and the invulnerable – and this is not the only way to see the evangelistic challenge!

Sharing our faith

These concepts of what evangelism is need to be subjected to analysis, because through such thinking we have in a sense driven away the very people we were meant to be helping. In the light of the need to reassess how we see our mission to those outside the Church, it is much more preferable to work with the New Testament picture of the Church and its calling as salt and light. From this model below you will see that, rather than being seen as an overwhelming institution that tries to convert by powerfully imposing its ideas on others, the Church is seen as an abiding presence. Instead of attempting to cure, reform or rescue people, we seek to build non-confrontational relationships with them which attempt to offer guidance and purity, but in an attitude of respect and mutuality, where listening is as important as speaking and personal involvement stands in the place of impersonal action.

Model	Church is seen as	Unbeliever is seen as	Christian needs to
Salt and light	Presence	Contemporary	Relate to

We are far more likely to see people as equals if we see our role as working among our contemporaries to further the work of God in their lives. The Church in this age should not see itself as the sole means of rescue, but as those who are called by God to work with him towards a common goal. A better alternative to seeing ourselves as beggars telling other beggars where to get bread would be to see ourselves as sharing our own bread without them knowing straight away that this is what we were doing. As our relationship with them grows, they will usually become more curious about the source of the bread and subsequent conversations can lead us on. We are the servants of society rather than its masters; we are contemporaries to our peers, not their emancipation; and instead of working *on* people, we are working *for* them.

The state of play today

It was an experience that I had as a minister which drove me to rethink the evangelical gospel and which highlighted the inadequacies of my own approach to evangelism. A large number of Sudanese refugees had come to live in our town due to the hostile political situation in their own country. Since they were Coptic Orthodox Christians (not to be confused with the Protestant and Roman Catholic traditions in Sudan, which arrived there only about one century ago), they did not quite fit into the neat evangelical categories of what makes a Christian, and so they became prime targets for the Town Mission and for many zealous pastors, including myself.

In our church one of the ways to reach them was to set up an English language school, as they badly needed to learn English to cope in our country. It was relational and practical and would provide us with the connection that we needed to see them truly saved. It was set up in our church, and I became one of the teachers.

Having got to know several of them fairly well, I was surprised by the faith that they already had – it seemed so real, so like mine. Yet, of course, they did not use the same phraseology – there was no talk of conversion, no activist streak, they did not quote the Bible all the time, and their prayers seemed more passive, lacking a sense of campaigning or crusading for truth. I talked to one of the other Christian leaders who was also working with them as an evangelist and told him how I felt. 'Well,' he said, 'they do have a faith, but it is not a faith in Jesus alone. They place an emphasis on the Saints and attach importance to pictures and statues.' I went away convinced by what he had said. The Bible says that there is salvation in nothing else and no one else apart from Jesus, there is no other name under heaven by which men must be saved. It is faith in Jesus alone which saves us. We must forsake all supplements and additions. I decided that they were not really saved because they had added on other things to their faith in Jesus.

I went back and talked this through with my captive audience. 'Do you trust Jesus only?' I asked them.

'Yes,' came the reply.

'But you seem to attach a lot of importance to statues and the Saints. Jesus is the only way to salvation – there can't be any additions.'

'We do trust Lord Jesus only,' they said (I hadn't got round to the definite article in the lessons yet!). 'These other things are just a way of remembering him, like a photo of your father or your family, to help them stay in your heart.'

We went on like this, back and forth. In response to everything I said they demonstrated a real and practical faith – undoubtedly different from my own, but genuine and full of love and humility. And what made it even worse was that they also had respect for my own understanding of the Christian faith!

On further reflection, as the years have gone by, I have realized that the 'filter' of my evangelical thinking was screening out everything that did not 'fit'. I thought the way of salvation was clear-cut and precise, almost like a mathematical equation – if you didn't get it exactly right, then it was wrong. This and *only* this was the way of salvation.

Despite the tremendous changes in the way we do our evangelism, it is still generally thought that 'sharing the gospel' and 'coming to faith' means explaining and believing the doctrinal content of the faith. This will vary naturally according to different approaches, but it will invariably include the person and work of Christ; our sinful condition; the need for repentance

and faith; and justification by faith alone in the death and resurrection of Christ. And becoming a Christian is equally thought
of as a heartfelt assent to these beliefs, whereby the person
places his or her faith in the Jesus we have told them about. This,
whether it happens suddenly or over a long period of time, is
identified as a conversion in lifestyle and attitude. We evangelical
Christians usually only accept a person's coming to faith in Jesus
Christ as 'real' if they have done so in a way that meets our
terms and requirements.

If people do not respond positively to our evangelical agenda,
we see this as their rejection of God and therefore their acceptance
of an empty, unfulfilled life. Only God as presented by the evangelical Christian can fill that 'God-shaped hole' in a person's life.

The word

The emphasis in evangelism is hence on the spoken word. The
gospel is viewed mainly as something that we share in statements
or propositions, and the response to it must be with heart and
mind, and must eventually result in similar beliefs being owned
and spoken about. Such an evangelistic proclamation of the
gospel is seen to be bold and the hallmark of a zealous church.

This is further emphasized in the recent and much-needed
attempts to de-jargonize our explanation of the gospel. Whilst
this is to be welcomed with open arms – and, indeed, should be
taken even further – it misses the point, in that it implies that not
using jargon and explaining the gospel to people in user-friendly
terms will make our attempts at evangelism more effective.
Really this is still the same old thinking that sees the gospel as
something which must be 'proclaimed by us' to the other party
through the spoken word – the gospel is seen as a code of beliefs
that the person has to understand and accept, rather than something that can be told and accepted in other ways.

To see the extent to which this approach has influenced our
thinking, we need to look at the emphasis that we put upon some
of the following activities.

The place of preaching

When the evangelical preacher is confronted with people whom he knows are outside the Church, there is an irresistible urge to proclaim the gospel. Tony was an absolute giant of a preacher! At one funeral service that I was involved with, Tony was to preach the sermon, and we had agreed beforehand that the kindest thing we could do was to lovingly and sensitively proclaim the gospel. Tony really went for it, telling the people in positive and up-beat terms that this need not be goodbye, because for the Christian there is the hope of resurrection and life after death. However, he went on to say in his forthright yet congenial style, that if they wanted to see this person again, it would only be possible by coming to faith in the Lord Jesus Christ.

One of the relatives afterwards came up and said to Tony that he 'sure did pack a powerful punch'. Tony saw this as a compliment, but I don't think the man meant it that way. I think he was very graciously saying, 'Is this the time to tell us this? And are you the right person to say this to us, the deceased's closest relatives?' I share the guilt of that occasion, and after years of reflection I can see that such an approach to proclaiming the gospel shows more respect for a belief system than for human beings made in God's image.

It is not just the mode of presentation that we need to look at more seriously, but also the content. Part of the evangelical gospel is the fallenness of humankind and the need for repentance and faith. Yet it seems to me that the way we choose to communicate this needs to be given our most focused attention. To communicate the rupture that exists between God and his creation is important, but some of the analogies that are used leave a lot to be desired. The story of the prodigal son is used to portray the idea that the unbeliever is living in the pigsty of life, far away from the Father, and needs to return to him. Or they are seen as lost sheep, and only coming to the Good Shepherd, Jesus, will get them back on track. Or they are said to be like one of the people in the Gospels who were healed by Jesus, and only by being healed of the pain and sorrow in their lives can they have wholeness. Once I even heard the lives of non-Christians being likened to a sewer!

Whilst there is some truth in all of these analogies which illustrate the plight of humanity in its separation from God, they must cause many people to wonder what it is that they are being asked to do. Whilst such inventive and graphic illustrations are to be expected from zealous and creative evangelists in their attempts to apply stories from the Bible to the condition of people who do not believe, most of the listeners do not value being told that their life is a mess, and in most cases it puts them off rather than turning them on. The very idea of people being separated from God is familiar to us but foreign to them; it is an informed Christian idea that means little to non-Christians.

If such preaching does not succeed in bringing them to faith there and then, rather than looking at ourselves we all too often create an excuse to get us off the hook. We say we have 'sown the seeds' that may well come to fruition in years to come. Whilst the gospel certainly does remain stored up in many people's hearts, such thinking on our part does need a reality check.

Open evangelism

Open evangelism is an approach that uses a wide variety of methods, such as watching videos or films, holding free town-centre barbecues, doing Sketchboard or magic in the open air, or using children's clubs as a means of getting parents to come to an end-of-term presentation where the gospel will be sneaked in. And yet we must ask how successful these activities really are. They undoubtedly produce some converts, but do they in fact do more harm than good? Do they not simply reinforce the negative views that many people already have about the Church and Christians? They are not won over by such activities because they have heard it all before, and it was not good. These evangelistic events are impersonal, they do not take the life-story of the listener holistically, and they are not relational. Also they often focus on the listener's 'sin' and 'selfishness' and their need to do something about their 'condition' – which are hardly issues that are going to gain much of an audience today. So by presenting the Christian message in an inappropriate way and so leaving people with a negative impression of Christians and the Church, this approach to evangelism actually makes it harder rather than easier to reach people.

Part of the reason why we evangelicals do this is that we believe that if we fail to preach the gospel, then we are little more than an unofficial equivalent of the social services, which means that we don't do much good at all. We are not called to practise a sanctified philanthropy; we are called to present the gospel truth. That truth is what really matters, and we are called to stand up for it, come what may.

And yet this approach needs to be examined, because if we keep on preaching the gospel in a way that alienates the people we are trying to communicate with, we have to ask some questions about the effectiveness of our methods. Some may feel that we should not stop preaching the gospel if it causes offence – the gospel will always receive rejection from people, as this is the nature of sinful man. We should expect to be vilified for preaching it – Jesus was, and so were the early apostles.

However, while we are not necessarily called to make the gospel palatable to everyone, we *are* called to make it persuasive (see Acts 28:23) and to do all we can to be involved in God's activity in people's lives to move them closer to him. For Paul this meant severely limiting his own freedom at times (see 1 Corinthians 9:19), and it may well be that we have to do the same.

If the cultural context of the day has shown us that certain ways of presenting the gospel message will not achieve results, then we need to think again. The presentation of the truth is not an end in itself; rather, we are to present the truth so that the hearers may embark upon a growing personal relationship with the God who is Truth.

One of the means of Grace is the Christian life (other means being things such as prayer, preaching, baptism and the

Eucharist), and if we are to enter into conversation with people about the gospel, we must first have lived it out in front of them. What is really important about faith in Christ cannot always be summed up in words. It has to be lived. In the past, according to different contexts, it has been appropriate to place the emphasis on the message of salvation coming through the spoken word, but in today's culture it is right to shift the emphasis to the Christian life.

Friendship evangelism

'Friendship evangelism' is the term that we now use when we are talking about evangelism that takes place within an already established relationship. We may get to know these people through work, or they may be neighbours, or we may have started church activities that are designed to help us make these friendships, like parents-and-toddler groups or coffee bars or listening groups. Friendship evangelism has now made considerable inroads into much of our evangelistic activity. There are now seminars, books and all manner of resources on how to make such social contacts and lead our friends to Christ.

This is undoubtedly a massive step forward, and certainly the future for evangelism must be relational. Here again, however, we need to look long and hard at our friendship evangelism and the motives behind it.

'Friendship evangelism' by its very name implies that the purpose of the friendship is to evangelize, that the goal at the end of the day is to witness to our friends. Our friendship with them is valuable, of course, but this value is fully realized only when we are empowered to present the gospel to them. The gospel is what gives meaning to the friendship. Without the call to witness, the relationship, from our perspective, would have little purpose. We need to be friends, but we must be constantly on the look-out for the God-given opportunity to witness to them.

However, this style of evangelism has itself come under pressure because it has not provided the numbers of short-term 'converts' that had been hoped for. Because of this the approach itself has come under criticism as being void of missionary vigour. Here is an extract from one writer's view of friendship evangelism:

We have tried to reconcile people and groups of people by using every gimmick and technique that culture uses to sell its automobiles, deodorants, civil repression and international warfare. We have tried surveys, group dynamics, T-groups, political activism, sociological and psychological processing, and all the well-known foolishness of church socials, retreats, picnics, bowling alleys, swimming pools, skating rinks, gymnasiums, counselling centres, marriage-and-the-family instruction, relevant ministries and updated theological schools – all pleasant, on occasion even controversial, but having nothing, 'absolutely nothing', to do with the mission of Christians as ambassadors of, witnesses to, what God has done for all men in Christ.

Looking at motives

The critics say that friendship evangelism is, in effect, the Church being sneaky. However, it is the motivation and expectation behind it that determine whether this is the case or not. If our friendships are seen as concealed evangelism with the expectation of a Christian conversion, then we will see such friendships as having failed. But if our motives and expectations are other than this, we will see things in a different light.

Our friendships need to be shot through with authenticity and integrity, or else they will soon wither and die. If we only give lip service to the notion of friendship, then we can be open to the charge of being sneaky, of only wanting to 'bag them for the Lord', but disguising it with a social camouflage.

Whilst Christians can affirm the place of friendship evangelism, we do need to be prepared to modify the way we think about it, to get a fresh perspective. We should not see the relationships that we build with people merely as a means of earning the right to tell them what we believe. Rather, we should see a relationship as something that has value in its own right and has more to do with who we are and the sharing of our lives and our love.

'Friendship' will entail a greater acceptance of who people are and a willingness to allow their response of faith to be less well defined. Witnessing to friends, family or social contacts is not the focus and zenith of the relationship; the high point is having them as friends, being in relationship with them in the first place. When our expectations are purely about friendship and servanthood, we cannot possibly see our efforts as having 'failed'. We will see them that way only if our objectives are defined by the narrow criteria of insider/outsider, believer/unbeliever and converted/not-converted. Our friendship, care and support for people should be seen not as a supplement to the 'real task' of winning them for God, but rather as an essential and unconditional response to the call of Christ on his Church to care for the least of our brothers and sisters.

It is the motivation and expectation behind our friendship evangelism that remains the crucial factor. Furthermore, quite apart from what it means to our own integrity, if we are carrying a hidden agenda, it will almost certainly be evident to these people and will most likely turn them off because of the hypocrisy of it all, supposedly in the name of Christ.

Not in word only but in power

It could be that the emphasis we have placed on 'speaking out' the message of the gospel in words is actually a *lack* of faith at times, rather than the bold faith that it is supposed to be.

Whilst in the process of moving from being a Pentecostal minister to being an ordinand with the Church of England, it was necessary for me to get work locally, and for this I needed to go into the secular world, working for a transport and packaging company. This was a huge step for me. I had been in full-time Christian work as a minister for 13 years. Also, whilst I had always been in touch with those outside the Church and had always been involved with them in social and friendship ways, I had not worked full time with people who were not Christians (in the evangelical sense of the word) for all these years.

My approach to working with these people was going to be the same as with all the other relationships I had built, with the belief that the most important thing I could do was to share my faith with them, share my whole life with them – warts and all – not just the propositions of faith.

For three months I kept quiet about the fact that I used to be a minister and I also avoided any opportunity of speaking about my faith. It is strange, but in that time many of the people there raised comments about spiritual or religious things – not in an overt way, but just in everyday conversation. For example, on one occasion one of my colleagues had just taken her kids to see the movie *Prince of Egypt*, the story of Moses and the Exodus from Egypt. She said that she almost cried as they crossed the Red Sea, because she did believe in 'all this sort of stuff'. I asked her if she went to church, and she said no, she didn't need to go to church to believe. Yet I avoided getting further into this issue because I knew that if I mentioned my own faith at that particular point in time it would have been too early, as I had not yet established credibility in her eyes. This decision was vindicated later.

I wanted to let my faith be expressed through my life, not in an attempt to convert them into what I expected them to be, but to share Christ with them in the most appropriate way. If this meant sharing the content of my faith, that was fine; if not, then that was fine too. I prayed that if it was right to talk about my faith, then God would provide the opening. It was not particularly on my agenda to speak about my faith, nor was I driven to do it other than if it came naturally in the context of sharing my whole life with them, of which the content of my faith is a part.

One of the customers who regularly came into the branch was someone who used to be in the congregation I had led, and on one of their visits they let it slip that I used to be their minister. The people I worked with were, needless to say, surprised, but they were also fascinated, and for the whole afternoon we were talking about the Church and God. They openly told me why they or their spouses did or did not believe, and they also told me about some of the personal hurts which they had lived through and which had influenced their beliefs.

The conversation was good-natured, and they totally accepted me and my beliefs because they had got to know me. They knew that I was not going to judge them, or try to convert them, or tell them they should start going to church and read the Bible. Yet if they had got to know that I was a minister before getting to know me, it would have been a very different story.

Saint Francis of Assisi said that wherever you go you should preach the gospel, and where necessary use words. Whilst the spoken word is extremely important, the emphasis in evangelism needs to shift to living authentic Christian lives, and sharing the gospel by sharing our lives and the values that our faith brings to us. It is ultimately in encounter with Christ that people are changed, and if we believe that Christ is truly in us and has shaped the way we live and see the world, then there can be encounter with Christ as we share our lives with others and live out our values before them.

If we decide that it is our life itself and the way we live that is the best evangelistic message, we can proclaim the gospel in words after we have done this, and we may be surprised at the impact that our lives have had on people. The life we live becomes the punch behind the proclamation, the muscle behind the message. I myself was totally taken by surprise one morning recently when I signed in for work and the man behind the desk jokingly said, 'We must be doing something wrong here. You always come in with a smile on your face, but most of the other guys come in here with a long, miserable face. What is it with you?' These were tough guys by any standards, and such a compliment meant a great deal to me. The smallest thing can take on a great significance when people notice something different about us and then discover that we have a personal faith in Christ. Winning them first by our lives is an absolute must in evangelism.

Authentic living is not about putting on religious graces to impress people with how Christian we are. Christ is seen more through the earthy reality of our lives and faith, warts and all, than through the man-made constructs of what we think being a Christian means.

Like apples of gold

When the time is right and we do share the gospel in words, we then know that we can do it with relevance to their lives. As we are told in Proverbs, 'Like apples of gold in settings of silver is a word spoken in right circumstances' (Proverbs 25:11). Evangelism must include the dogmatic content of our faith; we need an organized expression of our faith, or else it becomes shapeless and shallow. The word of the gospel is undoubtedly important, as by it we can help to clarify people's understanding of who God is and how he has worked historically to reveal his character and purposes. To influence people in living and acting we also need to influence them in their thinking, and to do this, presenting the shape and content of the gospel message, and indeed the values and insights that we Christians have, is extremely important. The spoken word in evangelism should flow out of our prayers for the people concerned and our care and love for them that has grown in the context of relationship, rather than being an automatic activity.

However, the gospel message cannot be limited to neat formulations; it should not be reduced to sharing the 'ABC of salvation'. The gospel points to the person of Christ and is multi-faceted. Properly understood, it invades every aspect of life.

An earthy gospel

In one of the conversations I had recently someone said they did believe and sometimes read the Bible, but did not go to church because they didn't think it was necessary, since they could be just as 'at home' with God when doing the gardening. I accepted this – of course one can be at home with God in the garden. I also accepted that one can believe and yet not go to church. In later conversations this person said that they just did not make the effort to go to church, but they would really like to. I said that I found going to church a beneficial experience, and in yet another conversation I said that church is not just a place that one attends or doesn't attend, but a place where a relationship with God can grow. In another conversation somebody else said that they loved walking by the seashore when it was blowing a gale because they felt cleansed by this experience. I asked them what they meant by 'cleansed'. They said that they didn't know how to define it, but it was something that they experienced. In another discussion this same person said they felt cleansed from all the 'grot' and the wrong things they had done. I asked them if the 'grot' was more than just wrong things they had done. Was it personal, was it an offence against someone else – even a someone else whom we may choose to call God?

If I add up these different conversations, I know that I have influenced these people in their thinking in some measure. The relationship is still intact and we can be totally open about our beliefs. Neither of us feels threatened and neither wants to convert the other into an itemized, packaged and labelled product.

The word of the gospel is still vital to our mission, but it must be spoken after first listening carefully to the issues that are the starting-place for this person. It must be done giving due weight to the value of our relationship with them in and of itself, and indeed to the place where we are at in that relationship. When we have listened carefully to the issues that are live for them, rather than speaking about the ones that are live for us, we need to think and pray about appropriate and relevant ways of helping them to take another step in their understanding and faith. We want to see them move closer to God, but we need to avoid defining what this is going to look like, and instead we should leave this to God. More of this in later chapters, but such an approach will require imagination and the ability to create opportunities when they are needed. Evangelism becomes dynamic rather than static under this model.

Call yourself a Christian?

Yet we should not be led into thinking that people will always gravitate to what we say and who we are. It is not as if we only have to live authentic Christian lives, and people will dramatically be awakened to new spiritual possibilities; as if we only have to be ourselves, warts and all, and they will see the light of Christ shining through us and will be led one step closer to him. On the contrary, it may well be that sharing our lives in honesty will highlight people's own insecurities and weaknesses. Quite apart from all the other factors, such as personality clashes, our weaknesses, our class, our education and our social status, which may well cause the other person to dislike us, we have to recognize that just being who we are is not always going to turn people on to Christ.

Some people can be so caught up with their own lives and opinions that they are unable to cope with anyone or anything remotely different. Our lives tell them of things that they do not know or understand. Our values are strange to them, challenging their preconceptions, their world-view and their experiences. We can become people whom they shun and avoid. No matter how hard we try to live out our Christian values in the realities of the everyday world, they will find fault with us and use this as a means of writing off Christianity.

Yet we should not see even this as a failed attempt at evangelism. If they have highlighted our weaknesses, we can use this to work on our failings and try to put them right. Where it is a need in them that causes the problem, we can only hope and pray that in time the light that we have will cause them to rethink some of their own values. This, however, remains in the hands of God. We can only do our best to live honest, loving, compassionate and authentic lives before them, and try through our own brokenness to reflect the wholeness of the life of Christ.

Chapter 3

OUT OF THE WHIRLWIND

The most beautiful experience we can have is the mysterious. It is the fundamental emotion which stands at the cradle of true art and true science. Whoever does not know it can no longer wonder, no longer marvel, is as good as dead ... It was the experience of mystery – even if mixed with fear – that engendered religion ... in this sense and in this alone, I am a deeply religious man.

Albert Einstein

It was out of the whirlwind that God called to Job and asked him: 'Who is this that darkens my counsel with words without knowledge?' What followed was one of the most powerful revelations in the Bible, and one of the most transformational experiences recorded in it. It was all done by asking questions and avoiding giving answers.

In our appraisal of evangelism so far we have noted that our evangelistic efforts have not really made the dent into our society that we would have liked them to. We need, therefore, to take a long, hard look at our evangelistic methods and to think about what it is that we are actually offering people when we evangelize them. What do we expect to give them, what will they go home with after they have been evangelized?

Do questions tell us more than answers ever do?

Much contemporary evangelism, though it comes in a variety of guises, is about offering a set of answers, a solution, a single way of sorting it out. The assumption is made that people's lives are unfulfilled in some way, or that they have various inherent unanswered questions, and that by coming to faith in Jesus Christ, as defined by those doing the evangelism, these issues will be sorted out.

The solution we offer may be by way of answering set questions which are imagined to be the sort of things that they need convincing about before they make a commitment to Christ, or, more generally, making Christianity out as 'the answer to life' – the panacea to their ills. Yet with such an approach, evangelism can become too closed and well defined – a set of solutions to problems and a range of answers to questions. Yet evangelism is not so neat and tidy. Bringing people out of darkness and into the light is often done with them kicking and screaming; like birth itself, conversion can be painful and messy. It is this notion of presenting evangelism as a set of answers, solutions and watershed experiences in people's lives that will be investigated in this chapter.

Could it be that by presenting evangelism as a set of answers, we limit people's genuine exploration? They will not go down a road where they see a cul-de-sac sign. Providing answers to questions, real or imaginary, may work for a small number of people, but it may also turn away many more than it lures. The reason for this is that people might not be as keen to find 'answers' as we like to think. They are not looking for cut-and-dried solutions, and the very notion of neat and tidy answers is perhaps far too simplistic for them, and they are certainly not expecting the Church to provide these answers. In a world that revels in ambiguity and refuses to take a stance, that is a pastiche of multiple styles and where there is a decided lack of answers, perhaps the provision of a single slick solution is out of kilter with the way people think. Perhaps people do not want answers in the way we think they do. Perhaps they are wanting the thrill of the chase!

Alternatively, rather than the answer, it could be the question which enables such exploration. It could be that in the very nature of the question – which allows people to find God for themselves in their own way – we find the most promising way forward for evangelism. Perhaps the question is more powerful than the answer; perhaps there is something in the nature of the question that enables people to discover for themselves. The theme of spiritual exploration that is prevalent in our society at this time (see Chapter 6) means that people do have questions, but they want to explore these for themselves. They don't want the answer – after all, if they found the answer, they would no longer have the fun of exploring!

Setting people free to explore means that we must rethink some of our evangelistic methods. It means that we should openly encourage exploration rather than trying to narrowly channel it. It means that our message will change from 'Jesus is the answer' to 'Jesus is the question', and that we won't pre-set questions that we want people to ask, but we will humbly seek to find out what their real questions are.

To those looking for answers …

… He gave only questions. When the Pharisees and Sadducees came looking for answers, Jesus responded only with more questions. When a lawyer came asking the way of eternal life, Jesus asked him questions about what is written in the law (Matthew 16:1–4; Luke 10:25–37). And there were other occasions when Jesus responded to questions by encouraging the seekers to explore their own questions, and he did this not by providing blueprints but by asking more questions.

The answers that evangelists try to provide are supposed to contain within them the essence of what it means to be a Christian. In other words, what the questions are and what the answers are provides the key to evangelism. When you find out what the answers are and believe them yourself, then you will be a Christian.

Real questions are from those asking them

But the reality is that all too often these are *our* questions; they are the ones that we have set, the ones we want people to ask; they are not *their* questions. They are not what most people are asking in their lives, and so they are inauthentic in the sense that they are not the questions of the enquirer. In this regard we are providing the right answers to the wrong questions.

Tim came to the barbecue with concerns rather than questions. He was interested in Christianity but felt that he could not live up to Christian expectations in the cut-and-thrust world of his work. He had listened to all the Christian answers about who Jesus was and how God cares for each and every one of us and the things that are important to us, but for him the hard issue was how he could be a Christian at work when at times he had to be fairly ruthless about goals, performance and so on. This was his concern; the others were not what really mattered to him. He was given some answers by some of the Christians present; others told him to chat to the Vicar; others told him that the church might be running a programme on 'How to be a Christian at work'. Yet none of this satisfied Tim, because the truth is that there is no 'way' of being Christian at work – there are no rules laid down for Christian ethics at work. There may be principles that we can try to live by, but there simply is no answer to this perennial question. The truth is probably that whatever answers there are, flow out of the Christian's personal relationship with God himself.

But what had thrown Tim off course was that he had been led to believe that Christianity was about a set of answers, and when he came looking for answers to his own real questions, there weren't any, and he went away disappointed.

What of the man who wanted an answer to the suffering of the innocent that he saw on his TV screen? Or the man who felt that evil was a malevolent force rather than a personal devil – a force that we can counter by becoming better people? Or the woman who had had an experience with what she described as a poltergeist and subsequently wanted to meet her guardian angel, but did not believe in God? Or the woman who felt more at home with God in her garden than in meetings with Christians?

Becoming a Christian should not be presented to people as a set of answers, as living by a certain set of predetermined standards. Rather, it is about embarking on a relationship with the Holy God and being transformed on the inside by that relationship, and then seeking to live out those beliefs and values in a Christian way. When we promise 'answers' and fail to give them, people go away dissatisfied. The real questions asked by the enquirer do not have such easy answers to them.

It may seem no solution at all to be saying that we should work with people in their questions without providing answers. But by being genuinely open to their questions rather than thinking that the solution always lies in our 'answer', we are possibly allowing them the chance to explore their own questions and setting them free to seek God for themselves. Understanding the nature of the question and how exploration works is key to this.

This topic will be explored now as we enter the story of Job to find a biblical basis for 'the question' which can become a way of exploring God and one's own spiritual identity.

There lived a man called Job

The first thing that we need to do is to take a very brief look at the response of Job's friends, because this is extremely relevant to the purpose of this chapter.

The central issue in the Book of Job that is relevant to our discussion is 'Why do people suffer?' It was the suffering of the righteous Job that caused the friends to offer their explanations of why this was so.

Whilst each of the three friends has a different approach, they all come from the same basic standpoint – that is, that Job's suffering is a result of sin. Man's fate is in his own hands; what he gets depends on what he does. Their arguments, whilst all having a slightly different hue, only colour the same presuppositions with an alternative shade. The belief of the friends that what you sow, you reap, affected the whole of a person's life.

For Eliphaz, no one is so righteous that he can expect to live a 'suffering-free' life. All mankind is sinful before God (Job 15:12–16), and it is clear that the righteous do not suffer (4:1–9). His argument is the same as that of the Satan in the Prologue – a self-serving ethic of earning a reward for works of piety. Bildad then enters the discussion, introducing the notion of cause and effect. Job's condition must have a cause, and this cause is sin. He says that it is because of the sins of his sons that this disaster has happened (8:3–7; cf. 8:12–13, 20). Zophar says that in fact Job's suffering could be worse; God has forgotten some of Job's sin, and therefore his suffering is lighter than it could be (11:4–6).

These answers given by Job's friends enjoyed a wide measure of acceptance in the community to which the Book of Job was addressed. In claiming to speak from tradition, Bildad demonstrates that his interpretation of Job's sufferings would have been the popular interpretation of the time. This 'tradition', furthermore, enjoyed an immensely long history in the Ancient Near East.

The problem with all this, though, was that not one of the answers satisfied Job in any way, and none of these answers is the solution offered by the book itself. What the friends say is criticized by Yahweh (Job 42:7), and the reader is left in no doubt that their approach has been unhelpful and even wicked.

The whirlwind cometh

Whilst interpretations of the Book of Job abound, most Bible teachers agree that the Yahweh speeches provide the key response to Job's suffering. Job had throughout the book been wanting God to speak to him; he had sought with all his heart to hear what God had to say on the subject of his suffering (Job 23:3, 5–6). After all the words of the friends, Job's last word was still to appeal to the Lord himself to come up with an answer (31:35). Eventually, at the very end of the book, out of the whirlwind, Yahweh responds to Job. The confrontation is not what Job had asked for, and it does not directly answer his questions, yet, most remarkably, Job is satisfied with this response!

So what was it that Yahweh did when he responded to Job's questions? Job has throughout the book been wanting an answer, and what does Yahweh do but come up with more questions! What was it that Yahweh was wanting to achieve in subjecting Job to this array of questions?

The very fact that Yahweh insists on asking questions rather than giving direct answers suggests that there is something in the divine question that judges both the questions that Job has asked and the answers that he has come up with.

The questions asked by Yahweh seem to be irrelevant to the main issue raised by the book: Why has the righteous Job suffered?

> *Where were you when I laid the foundation of the earth? …*
> *Do you know when the mountain goats bring forth? …*
> *Is it by your wisdom that the hawk soars? …*
>
> Job 38:4; 39:1, 26

Nevertheless, these apparently irrelevant questions provide the key response to Job's suffering, and ultimately lead him to repentance, satisfaction and restoration. There is in the very nature of the 'question', and particularly in the questions asked by Yahweh, something that causes Job to reconsider the mystery and complexity of the world created by God, and his own part in it. Questions can be a powerful way of making statements, and they are often the way chosen by God to enable the free thinker to make sense of his or her own questions.

We see this notion of the question being used to lead people to a greater understanding of the truth elsewhere in the Bible.

In Isaiah 40:12–26 the purpose of the questions regarding creation is not to derogate the people of Israel but to reassure them of their special status, their deliverance, their permanency in the divine mind, and the security of their relationship with him. As sole Creator, Yahweh's questions show that he exercises executive rule of the world and of all the events therein, and they expose the impotence of rival deities.

In Isaiah 28:23–29 the questions are taken from the world of agriculture to demonstrate why judgement had fallen on Samaria and why it must fall on Jerusalem also. Isaiah, in similar Socratic style, asks some questions: 'Why does the farmer plow the field only for a limited time, why does he beat dill with a rod but crush grain for bread …?' The questions are intended to prompt Israel to understand that each type of crop is gathered in a different way; the wrong treatment will spoil the crop. Just because Samaria was destroyed, doesn't mean to say that Jerusalem will be; God has a special plan for Judea that will end not in destruction but rather in restoration.

Jesus himself, when people came to him asking questions, would frequently reply with questions, and would often initiate them himself (Luke 10:25; Mark 11:29; Matthew 22:41; Mark 9:16). Often this would either silence those who impugned him or would make the enquirer go away with considerable food for thought.

By being asked these questions Job is moved to bow in awe before a mysterious God, but he is also made aware that in the very asking of the questions, God had invited him to consider the implications of the things he knew so well. This experience of education not only gave Job a new and deeper understanding of the ways of God, but also a dignity he had previously not known.

But how do the questions do this?

The paradox of divine justice

The questions asked by Yahweh provide Job with insights into things he had previously been unable to consider. They provide him with a divine viewpoint beyond his limited understanding, and show him the extent of God's rule in comparison to his own limitations. Whilst he had previously acknowledged God's omnipotence, it is only when the outworking of this is explained in the language of the world he inhabits that Job realizes the paradoxical nature of divine justice.

Within a short reach of some well-poised questions and with a few strokes of the divine artist's brush, Job is shown the mysteries of nature (Job 38:34, 39; 39:1, 19–20, 26–30) and his inability to control the seeming chaos of creation (41:1–8, 25–30). Yet whilst all this is beyond his ability to control as a man, the questions allow Job to appreciate afresh the wise management of the world by God (38:25 – 39:30).

In presenting the animal world, we have some 20 creatures mentioned, all of which, except the horse, are non-domesticated ones, and therefore beyond the control of man. There is no mention of sheep, ass and camel, animals which Job possessed in abundance and understood. The world presented to Job is the world in which beauty and cruelty exist side by side. The splendour of the bird mounting up to the heights is set alongside a description of it stalking prey, with its young ones soaked in blood (Job 39:26–30). Splendour and suffering are inseparable; they live and co-exist together. Alongside the splendour of the natural world we have its irrationality; with its order goes its disorder. So with the ostrich, a bird from which God has withheld wisdom; it displays no recognizable traits of wisdom as human beings would observe them, yet this is Yahweh's intention and it is marvellous (Job 39:13–18). The same point is made in Job 38:25–27 regarding the rain and the dew which water the desert where no one lives. They make it blossom, and no one sees it. What's the point of this? Perhaps God wants to create something beautiful in itself, and not for humankind.

Job is asked about much that is beyond his control, about that which threatens his existence. Innocent suffering makes no sense to Job, for, like creation itself, it lies beyond the compass of human power.

This paradox of divine justice extends into the moral world also. 'Will you make me out to be evil, to sustain your innocence?' calls Yahweh (Job 40:8). In Job 40:8–14 Yahweh's questions to Job put him in the place of divine power: 'What would you do if you had all power over all the wicked?' If Job were to crush all wickedness and injustice, would he be pleased with his totalitarian world of unilateral power? Would such an approach be better than the one chosen by God? In Job 38:13 God said that he is the one who brings the light that shakes the wicked out of their place. God does control evil, but in his own time and way. Job cannot regulate the time of evil or cut it short as Yahweh can, and if he considers that a divine concern for justice means stamping out all injustice, then God taunts Job to do just that (40:10–14). True justice deals with wickedness in other ways than brute force. God has deliberately worked contradiction into creation, and this is precisely what Job has been asked to explore in his own thinking.

The questions enable Job to see the power and righteousness of God. Job had built his own ideas of what order was and how it functioned on supposedly self-evident rules of justice and goodness, and yet the order that God has designed is infinitely more complex than this. God shows Job that his own experience of suffering has taken place within a world where what seems to make perfect sense doesn't always do so. His suffering has been part of this, and he gains a sense of satisfaction only as he learns to come to terms with God's rule in the world, and the call that God has placed on his life not to necessarily understand it all, but to live through it all in faith that God knows what he is doing. The questions are not answers, but they do enable Job to consider and contemplate those things in the world which tell us of our place within a world that is beyond the scope of human control.

It was only as God offered to Job some tools to do this that satisfaction and contentment came to him. The tools he offered were questions that were right at the heart of the issues that Job confronted.

Tools for today

As we walk with people with their questions, whilst setting this in the context of our relationship and involvement in their lives, we seek not to provide answers but to offer them certain tools to do this. The tools will vary with each different situation, and it is important here that we think carefully about the issues that we feel are the ones that we can build our values into.

We must not think that offering people tools to explore their own experience of mystery, as Einstein expressed it, is done simply by asking them questions. The nature of the question is used simply as a metaphor to demonstrate the open-endedness of spiritual exploration. If we offer people the chance to explore things for themselves, the sense of satisfaction that they will have in the answers that they find will be that much greater.

The tools we offer will vary with each different situation, as indeed Yahweh's questions suited Job. It is here that it is of great importance that we think carefully about the questions that people have, and what the underlying issues for them are.

Discernment

Lucy believed in reincarnation. She believed that the way we live in this life affects the way we come back in the next. She herself had had a lot of experiences of the *déjà vu* variety, and to her the simplest explanation was to believe in reincarnation. As I explored this issue with her, it was apparent that this person believed in the spiritual realm, she believed in the supernatural, and she felt better whenever she happened to visit a church for whatever reason (e.g. baptisms, weddings, visiting as a tourist).

As I listened attentively and keenly as she explained her beliefs, I did not feel that it was right to pick up on reincarnation as an issue itself, and I did not say that it was wrong. I asked her about these experiences and asked her how she explained them. But to help her to think it through a bit more, I honestly told her that whilst I did not believe in personal reincarnation as such,

I did accept that the world is connected spiritually in some way, both to previous generations of people who have lived and to those alive now. I said that when I die I will not come back as something or someone else, but when we are alive we can be influenced in a spiritual or supernatural way by others who have lived before us. Her experiences could be alternatively understood not as personal reincarnation of humans but that the whole of humanity is connected – we have a spiritual identity that can be touched and, indeed, shaped by those who have lived before us and those who now live alongside us. They are all part of the human story and we are all connected in some unexplainable way.

This, to me, is a Christian explanation that fits with some episodes in the Bible. Christianity understands faith as an historic thing that is handed down through the generations and has an historic basis (Ephesians 2:20). It also accepts that spiritual well-being and prosperity can be influenced by previous generations (1 Timothy 1:5; Exodus 20:5–6); that prayer is something that can cross boundaries of time and space (John 1:47–48; Luke 22:31); and that a person's calling exists before their birth (Luke 1:44; 2:26; Jeremiah 1:5). This demonstrates, at least to my satisfaction, that we are not just isolated islands living only in the here and now. We are an historic people, and what has gone before us can be an influence in the here and now. This is not necessarily bad or evil, as many would contend (although it certainly can be). It is part of what it means to belong to the evolving human community.

Some Christians may disagree with my thoughts on the subject; that is a healthy thing, and I accept that there are other tools that could have been offered to Lucy in this situation. Be that as it may, my purpose in this exchange with Lucy was, by offering my own thoughts in an open, exploratory manner, to make her think through issues that she may not have considered, which in turn would influence the way she looked at the issue. She did not suddenly stop believing in reincarnation, but she did pound me with questions about all sorts of things, as did the other person listening to our conversation, showing that I had awakened an interest in them both, and that what I had said had got them thinking. This discussion not only provided an alternative way for Lucy to interpret the events in her life, but also caused her to think more deeply about beliefs that were comparatively superficial and based mainly on her life experiences and on a popular awareness of reincarnation as a belief. In offering tools to Lucy, she was taken deeper in her own quest for spiritual beliefs, and afterwards she readily acknowledged that she was exploring and thinking about all these sorts of things at this time in her life, due to personal and family challenges that she was facing.

If we can be secure enough in ourselves to not feel that we have disowned our faith or deserted the Lord by being genuinely open to other people's exploration, then we can be a legitimate and meaningful voice in their exploration.

In seeking to offer tools to people as they explore their own experiences of mystery and paradox – experiences which may well lead them to be more in touch with the spiritual side of life – discernment is going to be a crucial factor. As we identify certain issues in people's search, it may well be that there are only some aspects of their beliefs that we feel we want to pick up on – ones that are most appropriate to bring them to a greater knowledge of those things that God, in Christ, has revealed to us. Some questions we will simply have to leave with them and let them explore by themselves.

We may feel that some of the issues we are confronted with are beyond the extent of our knowledge and understanding to deal with. We are not all called to be theologians or contemporary prophets. Yet this is part of the risk involved, this is part of being willing to embrace a new way of thinking about evangelism, and it is only by listening to them with one ear, and by gaining a deeper understanding of our own beliefs by listening to God and to fellow believers with the other ear, that we can do this. We do not have to be experts, but we can, in our willingness to avoid offering slick answers, help them to think through their own questions, and by being prepared to learn from them and from the whole Christian community, we can discover how to provide an exciting testimony to a living God in an original and contemporary way.

It is in such willingness that the future of evangelism lies.

A personal God

For many today even the notion of God is somehow confused. Many people are far more happy believing in the supernatural and the existence of evil forces or spirits than they are about the idea of a loving and personal almighty God. What is particularly noticeable about people's beliefs today is that they tend towards being spiritual but impersonal, whether it is dream interpretation, alternative healing, Feng-Shui, Tai-Chi or astrology, to mention but a few of the current elements in popular alternative spirituality. Yet it is precisely into such impersonal ways of seeing spirituality that we can be a balancing voice that speaks of a personal Creator God who is at work in all things and over all things and through all things (Ephesians 4:6). In living with these areas of spiritual quest and helping people to explore the questions that arise from the search, we have to accept, however, that this is the starting-place for many, and it is precisely here that we too must start if we are to help them move closer to God.

On one occasion I was talking to someone at work who had had a nasty experience, where she claimed that she actually heard a spirit talking to her and threatening her. She was very frightened by this, but managed to pluck up enough courage to go back and tell this spirit to go away and not come back. Apparently, to her knowledge it has not returned since. She was very frightened by this experience and went to talk to a Vicar about it. As a result of this experience, she had learned to stay away from all sorts of spiritual things, ranging from Ouija boards to churches.

She said that she didn't believe in God as such, but she did believe that there was 'something out there'. I asked her if she believed in the supernatural, and she said she did, both good and evil. Whilst she did not want to 'play' any more with the spiritual (i.e. Ouija boards), she had heard that if you place a white feather in your house, then your guardian angel will visit you. I encouraged her to wait for her angel and told her that when she did meet him/her, she probably would not know it and would only realize that it had happened afterwards. She said she had heard this also.

I also simply said that I believed in good and evil, and accepted that there are a lot of things – like her experience with this spirit – that I cannot explain, that are mysterious. However, over and above all of this, I believe in a good and loving God who remains in charge of his world. An exchange followed, and we talked a lot more about the idea of spiritual realities – the presence of good and evil, and the fact that God himself cannot be fully understood. As the discussion came to an end, she did accept that when all was said and done, she probably did believe in God, but had not thought of God before in the terms that I had explained.

She did not fall down and ask Jesus into her heart, but by offering to her some tools that enabled her to see that her experience had opened up to her the reality of the spiritual world, she was now able to understand a little better that, whereas before she had believed in some impersonal 'something', now the notion of God was clearer to her. This experience of something which could not be explained was a starting-place for her belief in God, and I know to this day that she continues to search very powerfully for spiritual meaning. It is this experience of mystery mixed with fear that has led people into religion, out of which has come the idea of God, who to Christians is a loving and personal Creator and Lord.

It is only if we love both God with all our hearts, minds and souls and also the people that he has made that we will be bold enough to step out into a way of evangelism that values exploration and people enough to set them both free!

Chapter 4

RETHINKING REVIVAL

The Church must be conceived as the place where man can get a taste of his eternal eschatological destiny which is communion in God's very life.

John Zizioulas

In the early 1980s, at just about the time when I was really finding my way into the evangelical and charismatic Church, there was a tremendous sense of the imminence of revival. In my late teens I remember talking excitedly with my friends and my brother after attending meetings absolutely burning with a sense of awe and expectation with the growing awareness that God was about to move in power to bring about his revival purposes. These were tremendous times that helped to form a lasting passion and zeal in us all to see God's Kingdom come. During these days, soon after my conversion, I began to realize more and more that God was powerful, that he loved his world, and that his purpose for it was to make it a place where he would be worshipped, where his plans would be followed and where his name would be revered rather than blasphemed.

The promises that these meetings made were powerful; they spoke of all sorts of glorious things happening. They gave me hope – hope that large numbers of people would come to personal faith in Christ; hope that amongst these numbers would be my friends, my family and my work colleagues; hope that the values of the nation would be changed and righteous standards would be upheld by the leaders and the people.

I have been to scores of meetings like this since then, and these long-awaited expectations have not been realized. I have spoken at some of these meetings, and even after those meetings revival still did not come!

In the years since then the promises have been re-envisioned and the time-spans have been lengthened. Some have claimed that revival has come, some have gone silent, and some still await it. For countless others, though, including myself, the type of revival that was expected seems to have eluded us.

It is in this light that revival needs to reconceived and the nature of God's plans need to be re-examined.

The good ol' days

In those exuberant and expectant days, revival was invariably presented, and still is, as an updated version of what revival looked like in years gone by. In fact, revivals of the past have been studied and the facts and figures have been presented in sermons and Bible studies to show what we should be expecting for today. I once held a seminar on the Welsh Revival as part of a study on revival. I talked about the large number of converts in such a short period of time, the scenes of mass singing, the powerful stories of lives changed, the social transformation that resulted, and I suggested that some of these things were what we should be looking and praying for when revival hits us the next time round.

Revival is still generally understood as God changing the world by displays of power through the Church. It involves getting people into the Church, and as they, in large numbers, change their lifestyle and values, this in turn means that society itself will change. Revival in seen as something that God will do by adding people to his Church. Revival will come when vast numbers of people come to faith in Jesus, but in a way that actively involves the Church and the inclusion of these people into the Church. Not only will there be large numbers of converts, but there will also be displays of supernatural power that will make the ungodly world sit up and take notice of what is going on. After God has blitzed the world, the 'world out there' will look like the 'world in here'.

This attitude has often been packaged in a 'holding the fort' mentality, with the world being seen as in a terrible state and the Church hanging on to the only bit of truth and uprightness that's left – a beleaguered minority getting smaller, with our only hope being the prospect that the power of God will restore us to our full number. Alternatively, there is the Kingdom triumphalism that has emphasized a mighty Church marching to transform the kingdoms of this world into the Kingdom of our Lord and his Christ.

The packaging may have changed, but the thinking about revival is still the same.

Yet this approach to revival, far from being a good thing, can actually detract from the major challenge that confronts the Church. It encourages us to think of revival as a quick-fix solution to the problems as we see them. As a Christian community, we have built up our own sets of values and beliefs, and we want revival, in one fell swoop, to restore these values to the world. This emphasis on revival in a large part of evangelicalism is in many ways a stark admission that we have so lost touch with our world that only something supernatural can help us.

The gap between the Church and the world is large enough as it is, and if the way we think about revival opens up that gap even more, then it has to be seriously questioned. In our meetings we sing and shout and comfort ourselves with the heightened rhetoric that God is a God of power who is moving in the Church and in the world to restore the glory of his name. This emphasis on what it's like on the 'inside' – the focus on worship, experience, our beliefs and practices, our view of what God is like – means that the gap that exists between the Church and the world keeps on growing.

Whilst there is nothing wrong with enjoying being a Christian and belonging to the Spirit-filled people of God, such an internal focus can have a tendency actually to weaken the Church rather than strengthen it, in that this weight of emphasis means that all our energy goes into our own fixed agenda – an agenda that has very little to do with the state of play in the world outside. Our relationship to that world is part and parcel of our existence.

Such an approach to revival has nothing to do with some of the abuses that can and will happen in any genuine movement, but we need to re-examine what we call revival, and think of as revival.

Revival is meant to involve the activity of God in his world through the life and witness of the Church. It is this aspect of revival that really opens up possibilities for us in an evangelistic framework.

So if revival is to happen, what form will it take? Is it right to think of it as a 'repeat showing' from yesteryear, or will it be something very different from before? If revival as we know it needs to be redefined, what is the call to the Church in this?

Revival and change for the Church

In my study on the Welsh Revival I came across the fascinating story of two women who had been praying for revival for some time. They prayed fervently every week and got others involved in praying also. They prayed for several years, and revival did come. In 1904–5 revival came to the Welsh mining towns and villages in an unexpected way. However, these two women would go into church and find dirty, sweaty miners, with their filthy boots on in church, dirtying the pews and not smelling too good either. They were shocked and dismayed at this – all their prayers for revival, and this is what had happened! They were greatly perplexed, so they called their prayer group together and said that all these years they had been praying for revival, and this terrible disturbance had taken its place. This was an awful thing to happen in the Church. They must increase the fervency and frequency of their prayer meetings and pray even harder for revival.

Revival is mucky! And revival often comes in unexpected ways and in an unexpected fashion. It requires the Church to re-evaluate itself and its own identity. Yet a revival that tries to recapture yesteryear can end up creating a diversion in our thinking. It defines revival by what has happened in the past, and by what we now think we are comfortable with, and in so doing fails to be open to new ways of being and doing revival. Revival talk can in many ways be 'evangelism by diversion', taking us away from what we see as a hopeless situation getting worse, and feeding our own illusory vision. We cannot recapture past glories – they are gone for ever, almost like the recent attempt to restore Leonardo Da Vinci's *The Last Supper*. The original cannot be recaptured, and all attempts at restoration are only a palimpsest that do not show us the original face of Christ and his apostles, but only our own self-satisfaction, our own inability to let that which is dying die.

The promise of the Holy Spirit is that he will take the things of Christ and apply them in ever new ways through his Church so that there can be fresh application of that which is timeless (John 14:26; 15:26; 16:13). The Church as a community longing to be revived can choose to allow itself to be reconstituted by the Spirit, so that we can offer inspiration for society. Thinking about revival should not distract us from focusing on the job in hand – that is, being thoroughly involved in the world in which we live, and co-operating with God in his own purposes. We need to constantly re-receive a fresh application of this for each generation. The picture that Jesus gives is of people hard at work and carrying on their normal daily activities when he visits them (Matthew 24:40–41; 2 Thessalonians 3:10–12; 1 Thessalonians 4:11–12). Any talk of revival that detracts from this can be myopic and can mar even our best efforts at social change.

Revival past

Realizing that revival for today means a radical change in our thinking should not in any way devalue or detract from the vital and important role that revivals have played in shaping society and, indeed, the Church. Revivals as they have occurred in times past have helped to define the Church's own identity; indeed, they have strengthened it in times of weakness, or they have given it an emphasis that has been lost or forgotten. This, of course, is important in that, if we are not secure in ourselves, then we can be of little use to others. If we do not understand the power, forgiveness, mercy, extent and range of God's love – things which past revivals have helped the Church to experience and appreciate – then our involvement with the world will be considerably less than it should be. God's purposes for his Church and his world are so great that it is naive of us to think that we can capture all this in one movement. It is so multi-faceted that it needs lots of 'moves' to capture it even in part. Revival has, in this sense, been part of these 'moves', helping us to understand aspects of God's character and his work in the world.

But we know this now – or we should do. If revivals in the past have helped to establish the Church's own identity, then revival in the future has got to be about defining the Church in relationship to others, about working with others to share with society all that we have learnt and all that we, the body of Christ, stand for. Now that these past revivals have helped us to be secure in our own identity, we can think of revival as a way of bringing our values and our character to other groups, not only to help them to emerge, but to help to create a better world of justice and equality, a world that helps people to strengthen their relationship with their Creator.

So, it is inappropriate to think of revival as revivals have been in the past. God does not need to repeat himself – he is the Lord of creation who is able to bring forth new treasures and apply in ever-new ways his story of redemption and salvation to his world. It is inappropriate to think that revival means that certain things will happen in certain ways as defined by revivals of a bygone age. It is also unhelpful to try to transplant the way revival happened in the 18th and 19th Centuries, or even in New Testament times, to today, and to expect the next time round to be the same again – a sort of 'Play it again, Wham!' Recent labelling of certain events and movements as 'revival' has fallen short not only of revival as defined by the New Testament, or even by 19th Century standards, but also of offering significant hope of a restored and dynamic Church that can embrace the society it seeks to win.

Revival future

And so we have to ask ourselves, What is revival? What is it all about? What is its purpose? If we take the pictures that Jesus gave of his people and of his Kingdom – treasure to enrich (Matthew 13:44), light to enlighten (5:16) and salt to preserve (5:13) – then the answer is that revival is about transforming people and society. In the past, and to some extent in parts of the world today, revival has accomplished such social transformation when large numbers of people have come to personal faith in Jesus, and when large numbers of people change the way they live, this in turn changes society. To build on this understanding means that revival is a call for the Church to be involved in the streams and rivers of God's purposes flowing out into the world, not to be a whirlpool of frenetic church activity that creates a false 'blessing' environment for Christians. Revival that does not help to create a society where God's purposes are reflected more and more, and where the people that make up society either embark upon or are strengthened in their relationship with God the Almighty, is not worthy of the name. It is a crying shame when all that the Church has to do to be considered as living in end-time revival is to laugh!

The Good Book

Part of the reason why we don't think of revival in these wider social and relational terms is that we have created our own hermetically sealed world which expects the world outside to look like the world inside. There are many reasons for this, and an analysis is beyond the scope of this book, but in wanting to suggest that revival should be thought of as the Church establishing and relating all that it stands for in a credible, relevant and dynamic way with others to help bring about a renewed creation, I would like to have a brief look at the way the Bible is understood.

The Bible is and should always remain central to our own identity and thinking. Yet if our study and application of the Bible is somehow detached from the reality of human experience it ceases to serve the purpose for which God gave it. If we allow our interpretations of the Bible to become so central to how we understand ourselves that we have forgotten to listen to those for whom we exist – namely, others outside the Church – then we do not do justice to its message. If our adherence to what we think is the biblical norm of revival and, indeed, what it means to be the people of God so removes us and detaches us from the world in which we are called to be a vital part of God's mission, then the world we have created becomes closed and myopic.

In such a closed world it becomes inevitable that we view others, even within the Christian tradition, with suspicion.

To work with others requires openness to them and also a security in what we believe and the way the Bible functions. If we feel threatened by having our views exposed to others' views, or by having the status, nature and authority of the Bible challenged, then we will be unable to relate to others with openness and with an inner certainty about our own beliefs.

In the evangelical world of which I am a part, the Bible, in a sense, is a symbol of whether or not we can be comfortable with such openness.

Having been involved in running several Christian training programmes, this has become all too clear to me. When I went to speak to church leaders who wanted to train prospective leaders in basic biblical skills, with an application of these skills to their work, ranging from youth workers to prospective deacons and elders in local churches, often they would view the teaching programme that I presented with some suspicion. This was nearly always because it presented ideas that were not in total agreement with those who were asking me to run the programme. In the case of training young people to be youth workers, it was dismissed with the notion that they didn't want their young people to experience what sometimes happens when people go to Bible college – that is, their faith is changed and challenged.

There are many examples of this, and here are two illustrations which will hopefully make the point.

The literal interpretation of the Genesis account of creation can run the risk of locking the application of biblical truth for today away in a small and fusty room, far removed from what most people take for granted – namely, evolution. This interpretation can at times be somewhat dogmatically asserted, and can be used by some as an evangelistic tool – that is to say, if we can prove that evolution is nonsense, then people will realize that there is a Creator and will come to a profession of faith. Yet such a view can polarize coming to faith. It is a big enough step for people to come to acknowledge the need for forgiveness through Christ, without adding that they need to throw away all that they have learned about science and evolution. A belief in evolution is portrayed as a destructive thing. I have heard several well-known Christian speakers say that this is the reason why people are without hope in today's world – because they think they just evolved from monkeys. Whilst the evangelistic nature of this book forbids a polemic on the matter, what remains important is that we do not make this issue – which is an area of disagreement even amongst evangelical Christians – into a stumbling-block for those whom we are seeking to move along in their growth towards God.

Another private world is the literal interpretation of hell. This may be an area of uncertainty and discussion, but if we insist that a person must accept this interpretation, we can create a barrier to their coming to faith. Again, we can polarize people. It is quite a big step for some to believe in an afterlife that is in some way influenced by this life, without having to take on board the specifics of exactly where or what hell might or might not be.

As Christians we are entitled to believe a wide variety of things on these subjects, but when there is an insistence on others believing the same as us, we can create unnecessary problems.

Evangelism from below

It is, however, in the field of biblical study itself that there has been a growing recognition that the Church needs to rediscover that people's experience can make a significant contribution to the way the Church sees things. The Bible itself testifies to the idea that we can only understand its message when we listen to God speaking through it with one ear and to the reality of people's experience with the other ear. The lives of those outside the Church become a text that sheds light on the biblical text; their story illuminates afresh the Bible story and becomes a filter through which the Church redefines its own self-understanding. Our Bible study is useful only when it can contribute to the life of the people.

The Good Book points us to a perfect person

Has the evangelical love of the Bible, which is one of our greatest strengths, become a diversion from an even greater truth about the Bible?

Bible teachers this century have suggested that the Bible is more of a dynamic story that witnesses to the life and death of a person than a set of factual statements or propositions; the book points us to a person. Truth ultimately rests in a person. Perhaps it is time that we evangelicals emphasized that the value of the book is in its ability to direct us to its author, and it is in knowing him that people find freedom (John 8:32). People come into truth by being in relationship with this person. The establishing of relationship is therefore essential to any growth of understanding or of living truth.

The rediscovery of relationship

Such an understanding of relationship means that the Bible, far from creating its own world that exists in isolation from the world outside, actually points us to the world outside! It points to Jesus, the Lord of all creation, who seeks relationship with all that he has made.

With this in mind, alongside the idea of revival we can see that the Church at work is a mobilized and active body that understands itself within the context of the whole society of which it is a part. It is the world, not the Church, that is the stage for God's creative and redemptive activity, and a revived Church is one that plays a key role with the Lord of creation in his concern for the final purposes of the whole of creation.

It is this very idea of relationship that holds open for us great possibilities in the area of revival. As the Lord of all of his creation, God has chosen to create a world that reflects his own relational being – that of Father, Son and Holy Spirit existing in a relationship of love and mutuality. The whole of humanity reflects the idea that persons seek relationships: we depend on them, are succoured by them, and we belong to them. Indeed, we only come to understand ourselves through our relationships. The extensive range of our social interactions produces in us as persons a wide spectrum of connections with other persons, from the anonymous relations with total strangers to the communal ties with certain others whose identities become thoroughly intertwined with our own. The connections we make with others are a central biographical theme for all of us. This is, in turn, a reflection of the kind of world that God has created – indeed, a reflection of the character of God himself. He has created the world out of his own generosity, and he reaches out to that world in openness for a relationship of love.

So taking this thought one step further, we see that God's work of salvation in his world can be seen in thoroughly relational terms. The Church as the body of Christ shares in this desire and purpose of God to be in relationship with the whole of his creation. Yet this does not just happen through individual encounter; it happens as the whole of humanity learns to relate to each other. There is something in the very act of relating to each other that enriches the world. Part of God's purpose for his world is not just that people come to know him, but, like any father who is the head of his family (Ephesians 4:6), that there is a restoration and growth of relations within the whole of that family itself. For our discussion on revival, society itself is that family. The destiny of humanity is bound up with God's purposes for the entire creation, and it is in this overall plan of working together that the Church has its own inescapable responsibility (Romans 8:19; 1 Corinthians 15:23–24; Ephesians 1:23).

The life of the Church, as that which touches both the world and the divine, is a sign of God's relational purposes. God is at work in the world. He seeks out its inhabitants, just as he seeks out his own lost sheep. He plans for them, just as he plans for those who know him by name. He is at work in their lives, whether they enter the Church or not.

Jesus is already at work in his world, whether we have got there or not, and it is precisely into this existing dynamic of relationship that revival calls us to throw ourselves. If those of us who are already enjoying a great relationship with God can form quality and informed relationships with those who exist within the larger scheme of God's activity, then that which glows dimly may be sparked to fuller life. When the nuclear family can embrace the extended family, there is healing for all. This is in stark contrast to a view of revival that is so internally focused that it fails to engage with others on a more mutual basis, and holds such a limited vision that it is in danger of becoming increasingly irrelevant. By following our own isolated trajectory we run the risk of becoming a dysfunctional family.

Revival is for the world, not the Church

If revival is about actuating change in our society, then this should not be seen as something that can only be done by getting people into the Church, although this, of course, is still important. Revival has got to be seen as something that the Church does by its own action and involvement in society, by bringing its own identity and values to other groups in society who are also proactive in change. If it is true of us as persons that we only come to understand ourselves in relation to others, then it is equally true that the Church will only understand itself in relation to others also. So what are some of the ways we can do this?

Entering the conversation of society

Society is not a static thing with a static set of values; it is a changing thing that moves and fluctuates as events occur and as the social, economic, cultural, political and environmental climate changes. It is a living thing that is shaped by events that occur and what we make of them and how we change because of them. This in turn means that the values that society holds will also fluctuate and move as we grow together through different experiences.

These values are constantly changing, and some of the issues that confront us as I write this book may have already passed by the time they are read, but they will have become an ingredient that adds mood and substance to society. So when society in the United States is filled with stories about the sexual behaviour of its leaders, this is a conversation that changes and adds to society's views. Or in the United Kingdom, the crisis – whether real or media-hyped – that resulted from the death of Princess Diana, and the comment that followed it, became a discussion within society as a whole that influenced the way people thought. In recent months the world has faced a moral and ethical crisis concerning 'ethnic cleansing' and military action, the United Kingdom has seen a spate of racially motivated terrorist bombings, and the United States has faced a wave of violent juvenile crime. Then there are the more general issues, such as racial and sexual equality, crime and punishment, commercial exploitative enterprise, and media and press activity – the list is endless – that shape the way society functions and the values it holds. People talk about all these things in agreement, disagreement, rage or antipathy, but they are all things that are a conversation at one moment, and become embedded in our cultural and social values the next.

To these and the multitude of other things that shape the values and trends in society, the Church needs to find ways of adding its own distinctive voice, such as local action, political action, social involvement, the use of the media and community work. Once we get the vision for it, the new ways of being and doing revival will emerge.

It may well be that for some of these issues the Church has nothing more to say. But in many areas the Church needs to be in a position to add its own distinctive voice to this conversation. To allow such talk to go unseasoned with the Christian voice, whilst we argue about what constitutes revival, hardly does justice to the concept of salt and light.

In some of these conversations the Church will need to work with others to bring about improvement. Revival as relating and working with others such as economists, sociologists, anthropologists, psychologists, physicists, socio-biologists and philosophers means that we talk with them so that together we can help an ever-renewed world to emerge. This, however, is not new. In every generation, Christians have been in dialogue with contemporary philosophy and culture, ranging from the early Church Fathers relating their theology to the ideas of Platonism, to the European post-war Church and its interaction with the existentialist comment on society. There is always the risk that such discussion becomes distorted, so that either faith or culture dominate each other, yet it is a risk that we must be willing to take. A revived Church is a Church that knows how to be both consoling and challenging to society, and also knows how to receive challenge and consolation from society.

Back to grass roots

So how do we connect such lofty thoughts with the grass-roots reality of being a Church for the people? This is not a small matter, and it is one that will undoubtedly challenge us. But we are not alone; we belong to the historic community of faith, which has always sought to enter the exchange in a meaningful way. We face the task of interacting with others in the Church and outside it to try to find ways of doing this.

Thought change

Paula was as outside the Church as anyone else I know. She was a great person – fun to be with, pretty broad-minded in her approach to life, and her sense of humour could often make me blush. But when she lost a close relative, it hit her hard. To my knowledge it did not prompt her to particularly try to make any religious or spiritual sense out of it – it was just another blow in her life that she was simply going to try to live with. But the one piece of sense that she did try to make of it was simply to slip into a church one lunchtime, just across from where she worked, to sit and be quiet and collect her thoughts. She had never been in there before and may never go there again, but for these few brief moments there was something about being in the stillness and atmosphere of a church that made her feel better. When she came back she told me where she had been, and said that it had made her feel better.

How we think of the Church and how we 'do church' will be influenced by developments in other fields of study, as well as being an influence back into those fields of study and society as a whole. For example, sociologists have recently focused on the importance of 'place' in our shifting, transient society. It is increasingly important to have a 'place identity'. Since World War II we have put less value on place and more value on mobility. Things like airports, cars and laptop computers have become symbols of our modern world. They show that we have valued exploration and devalued home.

Yet the emphasis in Christian circles can be that faith is about people, not places. We hear the oft-quoted maxim that the Church is people, not buildings. We don't want those outside the Church to think of it as a building; we want them to think of it as people. Whilst this is true, perhaps we need to take on board into our thinking what the sociologists are saying and what many people like Paula are saying.

Perhaps buildings can be sacred space after all. Perhaps getting people used to the symbols and atmosphere of a church is a good starting-place. Perhaps it is precisely the fixedness and the history of the building that appeals to our transient, rootless society. Perhaps this is an area where we need to listen to others and slightly change the way we think. This in turn will mean that we can reflect back into society what our church buildings stand for – their stories, their significance as a place of divine encounter, their testimony to all the people who have found in there a relationship with the living Jesus.

Local change

Two years ago I joined a local political party so that I could work with others to help to bring about a more just and fair society, where the values that I believe to be Christian can be fought for. The action of Christians and the very sharing of our life with others can be an influence in the areas of change for which we have a passion. We do not need to be political gurus, but if each local church were to encourage one or two of its members to get involved in a local political party, the impact could be considerable, not only in the realm of politics but also in helping the Church to stay ahead of the issues in our society as they happen.

My own local church was involved in a project which attempted to establish links with other groups in the area to build constructive and meaningful relationships with them and with the wider community. We talked with the local police, who have a community liaison officer whose role it is to build and work with others for the good of the community. We talked with health and social services visitors, who are often at the sharp end of needs within the community. All in all we spoke to about 10 groups, ranging form local publicans to school teachers, who helped us to find out about the needs of our area. It was discovered that one of these needs was to provide a low-cost listening and/or counselling service to a particular sector within the community who suffered from loneliness and depression. There were particular social and demographic reasons for this, and it was into this need that the church decided to work with other groups to fulfil the task.

This, then, has a twofold purpose. First, it is the church working with other groups and sharing its values with them. It also shares its life and values with the wider society in that local inhabitants get to hear of the scheme run by the local church. Secondly, it builds relationships with those who are counselled in a way that shares the values of the church but also shares the lives of the Christian staff regulating the project, bringing these people into contact with those whose faith is vibrant and contagious!

Another similar project was in a poor area where the only place for young people was the pub. The church, in conjunction with the local council, set up a cyber-cafe where young people, under regulated conditions, and getting them to take responsibility for the equipment (in the first year of the scheme none of the equipment was broken or vandalized!), could go and play on good-quality games. It was totally non-confrontational and did not lambaste people with faith, but was and is an agent for social change. It also builds relationship with people and shares the faith in and through the Christian life.

This is revival as relationship at one level. There are many more examples that could be given of this kind of working together with others to bring about a networking of relationships.

Social change

But there is also change needed at another level – in the very systems and values that make our society what it is. In addition to our prayers, of course, the Church could be looking for ways to influence the wider society in those things that we believe are important issues.

We can and should be involved in building a better world – a world where the quality of people's lives is affected by our own action and involvement. In some areas of wider social change, though, this can only be accomplished if we work with others.

Let's consider Roger and Susan. They go to work in the day, come home in the evening, have their evening meal together, relax and watch TV. As they watch, Roger gets bombarded with promises about products that will all enhance the quality of his life, whilst Susan gets bombarded with images of beautiful women and is told that if she buys these products she too can be this appealing.

Roger's wage in his local firm means that he can just, at a pinch, afford to do this. Susan, a driven career woman who compares herself unfavourably with other women, diets, buys and works so that Roger will not be able to make an adverse comparison.

When a new private firm takes over Roger's company, they cut the hourly rate from £7 to £4.50, and increase the working hours to 12-hour shifts. Roger cannot afford to take this drop in salary, and when he and others complain, they are told that if they don't like it, they can leave. When Susan's drivenness turns into chronic fatigue syndrome, she goes to the doctor, who puts her on a course of medication.

Because Roger is unskilled and cannot afford to resign, he stays on at the job because he has to. He regularly works between 30 and 40 hours of overtime each week to get a salary that he can live on. He is constantly tired and spends little quality time with his family. All this makes Roger unhappy, which he tries to rectify by more physical comfort and alcohol, all of which he cannot afford. His family are also unhappy because he is miserable, but also because whenever they do get to spend time together, Roger is either too tired or too depressed to really make the most of his family. Susan is depressed and needs to continue with her medication to help her.

They buy their Lottery ticket each week, dreaming and hoping that they will win, because if they do, all their problems will be over. This is now the great hope of their lives. They tell the people at work what they would do with the money if they won.

This may seem a simplistic and pretentious story, but the hard reality is that Roger and Susan are representative of millions of people who make up our society. If we blame them for their situation by telling them they need to spend more time together, or are wrong to buy Lottery tickets, or need to start going to church, it will only serve to make them feel even worse about their situation.

What has evangelism and revival got to do with all this? Isn't this for politicians rather than the Church?

If we rephrase the question, it does take on a slightly different light. What has revival got to do with a society that actively promulgates a winner-takes-all mentality that results in some people living these kinds of lives? What has revival got to do with a world where material gain and social comparison lead to depression and rejection, where people are reduced to economic statistics as the cheapest way of getting a job done? What has revival got to do with a consumerism that is such a part of society that people have to build their lives around a job that they do not like, in an environment that is destructive to their well-being, while a few other highly talented individuals amass vast personal fortunes? What has revival got to do with people feeling so unhappy and frustrated that they spend hundreds of pounds that could be better used so that they can live in a dream-world of winning the National Lottery?

If our evangelism does not address the savage competition and inequality that promotes such a dog-eat-dog world, then it fails to understand the mission of God for his world, and continues to follow an elitist pathway that will remain isolated from the real trends that make up most people's lives.

A symbol, not a photocopy

When I visited the island of Iona, the place where St Columba launched his mission into Scotland, I was struck by one of the illustrations made by the leader of the Iona Community. As we toured the island and stood among the ruins of the nunnery built over 1,000 years ago – a place of prayer and inner spiritual identity for countless people in the past – we noticed lying on the ground a Coke can. Here, in the midst of the ruins of a place of spirituality and communion with God, lay a symbol of our world today – a symbol of consumerism, pick-you-ups and personal image. The leader of the Iona Community said that with about a third of a million visitors to the island each year, he sees this over and over – people's spiritual identity lying in ruins, but at their feet the hallmark of empty, impersonal lives made up of individualism, personal pleasure and material gain.

In my introduction I suggested that the Church needs discernment to see the evil in society and to work for change, and also to see the good and to work alongside it. Yet in most cases we do not combat evil within the very fabric of society, either by reacting so strongly against it that we lose all point of contact with those who have fallen prey to its malevolence, or by becoming part of it, by imbibing it into our own life. What is called for is identification and involvement, but in a way that points towards a new and redeemed way of being. The Church in revival should not be another world, nor should it be a copy of this world; rather, it should be a symbol that touches both the world and the divine, a signpost that points to a redeemed humanity which will be realized in the conclusive purposes of God. To grasp this and all that it means is of vital significance in understanding this book.

People in other disciplines ranging from psychologists to economists are also concerned about such trends in society.

Some of the suggestions that they make will not always fit into the Christian ideal, but this must not be excessively reacted against, when many of their suggestions do provide some powerful and practical ways to help address some of the issues that I have raised here. We, the Church, should be working with and encouraging such visionary thinking that fits in with the overall mission of God for his world. We should be working with psychologists, sociologists, economists and politicians to help build a better world, rather than ballooning off into our own world of ideals where there is little connectedness with where the real issues are at.

Part of helping Roger and Susan to find their identity is to tackle the underlying causes in society that drive people to live like this. Surely the greed, hedonism and individualism of our society is what should be tackled.

What about the Church?

We would still like to see Roger and Susan start going to their local church, and we would still like to see them come into a dynamic relationship with Christ that becomes the key relationship on which their whole lives are built. But the expectation for this is not a short-term one. We will not 'bag them for the Lord' that quickly. There are simply too many hurdles out there to get over for this to happen. But if we Christians can get involved in creating a world where there are not so many hurdles, where the gap between them and us is not so large, and where 'church' has become part of their vocabulary again because we are part of what makes up their everyday lives, then it might not be too unrealistic to expect Roger and Susan's kids to start coming to church. We might even get to see Roger and Susan themselves some years down the line. There's no quick-fix revival any more. We must learn to take a long-term view of revival, where a revived Church is one that creates a world that is more conducive to the search for a spiritual identity and relationship with God.

Revival as openness

This, you may say, is great, but it does not mean that we should not still be working towards revival as it is currently thought of and as it has been experienced in the past. Many churches work for social change and get involved in their communities in all the ways suggested, and still seek for a renewal of their church and pray for revival.

Yet working with others means more than merely working with them in grass-roots practical ways. It requires a genuine openness to what they believe and also an openness to what the people with whom we have built these relationships believe. Expecting them to reorient to our values and to imbibe our way of seeing things will only lead to disillusionment in both parties. Relationships mean mutual change, not just a way of making others change to meet our requirements.

Such openness and what it means for us will become more evident as we explore other issues related to this in the following chapters.

Chapter 5

THE PILGRIM'S 9 TO 5

> We must take care not so to embellish the gospel ... that it is quite
> lost, to defend it so well that it collapses. Let us not be anxious,
> the gospel does not need our help; it is sufficiently strong of itself.
>
> Martin Luther

I have always liked the word 'pilgrimage'. It conjures up to me
the idea that we are constantly moving, we are continually progressing towards a destination at which we have not yet arrived.
It also speaks to me about a common destination at which fellow
pilgrims will also arrive, and yet their journeys to get there may
well be very different to our own. Yet despite these different
paths, all the pilgrims are progressing towards the same destination and will all have their different stories to tell of how they got
here and the events that befell them as they travelled on the way.

It also evokes the idea of changing scenery. As we continue
along our trek, things change, the landscape that makes up each
stage of our journey shifts from scene to scene. Each scene on
our journey has different characteristics that make us 'feel' very
different. As we walk by the seashore it feels very different from
when we walk by the gently flowing stream. The hills and downs
that we walk over give a very different sensation to the wooded
area where each step is a tussle with the surrounding bushes and

branches. So it is with people as we progress towards our final destination. We move through very different types of spiritual expression and experience. What we once held to be the greatest aspect of serving the Lord now seems 'everyday' as we serve him in new and different ways.

This notion of pilgrimage is, of course, very familiar to Christians. It was part of Israel's religious life in the Old Testament and has been written and spoken about much in Christianity. Yet this notion of pilgrimage can also be extended to other people as well – not just to other religious people but to people who appear on the surface not to have much religious or spiritual inclination in their lives. They too are pilgrims travelling along life's road, not just in the everyday things that make up their lives in general, but as spiritual pilgrims seeking identity, understanding and meaning in life.

With this in mind, evangelism today will mean recognizing that everyone is a pilgrim and has already made some sort of spiritual journey, and continues to make it. As Christians, therefore, our beliefs and our own pilgrimage will intersect their lives where there already exists movement and direction. They are not spiritually dead, as is often supposed by those who see conversion as the beginning of the spiritual life. They are not static stories but happening history. The pilgrim is everyman, the pilgrim is the person you sit by on the train to work, the person in the lift, the person in front of you in the supermarket queue. The pilgrim is 9 to 5.

Silent stories

For many people this pilgrimage is often well disguised and perhaps not talked about much in the superficial everyday conversation that we have at work, in the pub of an evening, or at the health club at the weekend; but it is there, it is an area waiting to be explored, and waiting to be given voice.

Joe, someone I worked with recently, was never one to get into conversation about some of these deeper issues. He would always ensure that the conversation was either to do with business or was risqué and superficial. Then one day one of our customers, who had just lost his wife tragically and was himself seriously ill, caused us to open up a conversation about death. Joe said that tragic death was not always a bad thing if you were religious and believed in something afterwards; but he didn't – he believed there was nothing, because he had never seen anything or had any experience in life that made him think there was. You could almost say his was a non-existent pilgrimage. Here he was, in his early forties, and was saying he had never in his whole life had any experiences that made him think that there was a God or that there was anything other than these few, painful, suffering years.

I left the conversation there, but came back to it some weeks later, and it transpired in what turned out to be a significant discussion that Joe really did want to believe in something but had no evidence. He almost felt that there should be 'something out there', but his own life experience would not allow him to believe this. He had often wondered about it, and had talked it over with others who shared his opinion and with others who didn't.

We must leave Joe to continue his own journey and, when the time is right, it is certainly hoped that the claims of Christ will be heard by him and will make their mark on his life. Yet whilst resolution to these questions may not fit our timetable, what it does tell us is that such thoughts about the nature of religion do take their place in even the most unlikely person. Perhaps the absence of experiences for Joe was the very thing that made the question present. Who knows? But whatever God's plan for Joe's life may be, I know he is on a pilgrimage and that he can grow towards God in the right situation.

For others, their pilgrimage may have sent them down a dead end, due to a tragic experience at a young age, where all that they believed was shattered. For others, it may be considerably more well developed, with an appreciation of the Bible, a belief in God and the supernatural, and a desire for their children to grow up with Christian values, but it is not itself expressed in any way that formally identifies with the Church.

Whatever the state of their journey, for most people life has involved mystery or complexity at some point – a bereavement, a disappointment, a dangerous or near-death experience, a concern about the environment, an illness that makes them try alternative medicine or evokes an interest in some of the other forms of spirituality currently manifest in our culture. All these things can be ways that cause people to think that these experiences have happened for a purpose bigger than themselves. In our discussions with them they may claim not to be religious, but the very fact that they are asking these questions, even raising the issue of religion, says in itself that these have been mystical events. We need to learn to engage with people on the issues that move them personally and make their life important and significant. As we bring our Christian values to these kinds of discussion, we can be imparting something of ourselves and therefore something of our faith. We can impart Christian truth without always having to make it overtly Christian.

Whatever people's experiences might be, they have in their own way contributed to this person's view of life and the way they live it. Some of these, we may well feel, could lead people in the wrong direction, but nevertheless there are areas in which people as human beings have realized that life is at times complex and things in it cannot be explained by science or reason alone. It is on these building-blocks of spiritual exploration in people's lives that we, the Church in our evangelistic mission, must be prepared to build.

Pilgrimage thermometer

I remember that years ago, with great Christian zeal, I used to go to work and try to talk to my colleagues about the Christian faith. Each time it seemed that my words fell on deaf ears. People were more concerned about building a life for themselves that was materialistic, hedonistic and gave little thought to some of the deeper issues of life. I always seemed to be the only Christian in the place. No matter how big the organization was, I never came across another Christian, or, for that matter, anyone of another faith. I used to long for someone to show an interest in even the remotest aspect of the supernatural or the spiritual. I used to try to get people thinking about things other than their materialistic lives and to think in other dimensions – usually to no avail, and usually to the detriment of my popularity.

Over the years there has been a gradual change, and going back into the secular work environment whilst an Ordinand with the Church of England has demonstrated to me that my zeal all those years ago would have brought very different results today. There is a more developed awareness of spiritual things in people, and there is a more open environment in which to air one's beliefs and to talk about the spiritual things or even the life and work of Jesus. Whilst this pilgrimage is, for many people, still in its very early stages, and is often submerged beneath a whole load of other cultural and social baggage, it is unquestionably there.

It is these encounters with the spiritual side of life that will become markers along the way of their pilgrimage, if handled properly by us. If we handle them well, they could well become signposts to God through Jesus, the One who we know is the key to it all; but if handled badly, they could become sticking points in their life, not only in growing to a faith in Jesus but to any further spiritual development.

If we can begin to see those outside the Church as pilgrims as well as those inside the Church, it is not a gargantuan leap to see that sharing our faith with people will mean that we do so in a way that identifies and relates to whatever stage of this journey they are at. This, of course, requires a great deal of thought, and is developed in other ways in later chapters, but here are some important starting-points to consider.

Cultural factors

Someone who worked amongst Japanese students in England once told me that he was able to lead many of them to faith in Christ. I was surprised at this, as I had previously heard that

Christianity in Japan was not particularly flourishing. When I asked him further about this, he said that when these students move out of their own culture and are able to explore life and, indeed, Christianity, from a different perspective than they had previously been able to do in their own culture, they were enabled to see it from an angle they had missed before. It was almost as if moving from one culture and world-view to another enabled them to get a slightly different perspective on life, from which they were able to express the faith that they did have in new ways.

This illustrates well, I think, the notion that no person just receives the word of God as objective truth. Each person hears and understands the gospel through the filter of their own personal situation such as race, gender, age, education, sexual orientation, social factors such as socio-economic standing, religious affiliation, their job, and cultural factors such as world-view, language and gender expectations.

Surrounding all of these aspects, every nation has its own life and its own story to tell. The life of the nation influences the way the people in it think, feel, behave, believe and act. We are not just individual islands that reach conclusions about such weighty matters as personal faith entirely on our own; we are children of our culture, citizens of our nation. The history of our nation moulds our own life's experience and shapes the way we perceive religion. This, when applied to the way people in Western nations see Christianity, has remarkable overtones. To suppose that people just arrive at a rejection of the Church and Christianity without hundreds of factors making up the person that they are, does not do justice to this notion. This is particularly significant in the Western world, where we have a long history of Christianity, but which is now thought by many to be post-Christian. They have been fed from day one with thousands of pieces of Christian heritage that have shaped the way they have viewed God and religion.

Other factors

People living in the Western world have had a great deal thrown at them in the last century – not only to do with all that Christianity has been through with close historical scrutiny and psychological analysis, but also from the scientific, industrial and technological challenges.

For example, a person living 150 years ago would not have been subject to things that people are today. They would not have been subject to the vast array of scientific developments now made freely available through the media, and which can be seen to undermine the idea of a personal Creator God. They would not have been subject to massive media hype that has emblazoned the hypocrisy and abuses of the Church for all to see. They would not have been influenced by the vast array of historical criticism that has been thrown at the Bible and especially at the life and person of Jesus. They would not have been a part of a society that has seen an almost complete privatizing of spiritual and religious issues. They would not have been so disoriented with the Enlightenment promises of equality, human reason, happiness and abundance, which have for today's seeker given way to disenchantment and doubt.

For sure, Westerners have been presented with much that has disoriented them with regard to their own pilgrimage.

Milestones along the way

To expect people to be able to instantly reorientate themselves when it comes to Christianity in the light of this is perhaps unreasonable. As much as we would like them to be able to step out of their cultural conditioning, they are not able to. Though we like to think that our clear presentations of the gospel should be enough for them, often they are not. We cannot cure all that they have been through with a presentation of the gospel and fervent prayer. The evangelistic challenge must be prepared to take its place alongside those to whom it is called to minister. We share their world with them and are called to share the good news with them in a way that recognizes their own starting-place.

It has been well said by many missionaries that culture shapes the human voice that answers the voice of Christ – that is to say, that it is partly the context and environment in which we hear the word of God that colours the way we not only hear it but answer it. The word of God does not just arrive on the doorstep of Ms or Mr Post-Christian one morning, neatly packaged and labelled 'The word of God for you'. It comes to that person within the context of their own heritage, social structure and prevailing belief systems.

The incarnation tells us that God's way of salvation was a taking on of all the limitations of what it means to be truly and fully human. It tells us that the Word of God came to us as a Palestinian Jew who wore Palestinian clothes, ate Palestinian food and spoke Palestinian languages. God comes to us as one of us. The Word of God descending into our situation comes dressed up in our guise.

This in turn means that a truly incarnational gospel will adapt itself to the limitations of people, simply because this is what the incarnation itself, as the very way of salvation, teaches us. It will also recognize that people may not be rejecting the Church or the gospel in as cold a condition as we think. We are called to relate to people in whatever condition they are in, just as God in Christ related to the world he was coming to redeem by sharing with it in its limitations. Such an approach endeavours to avoid some of the hallmarks of a confrontational religion that expects instant conversion and instant transformation, and is what is necessary if we are to make headway in evangelism.

'Post-Christian' is not atheistic

Part of what it means to be a pilgrim in our world today who is outside the Church and therefore a likely candidate for evangelistic action, is that these people – let's call them Sue and John – live in an environment that has a very long history of Christianity.

This, whilst perhaps obvious, does put a very different slant on our evangelistic efforts today, as compared to those of the early Church or the first missionaries arriving in foreign lands. Such a difference is worthy of note. When the Apostles and the early Church set out on their mission, the world was pre-Christian – that is to say, the fabric of societies, especially those that were not influenced by Judaism, was as yet unchanged and unchallenged by the radical and transforming message of Jesus Christ. Christian things lay ahead of them; their present condition was one untouched by Christian things; their future was one that would be. But for us, the gospel has been an intricate and intimate part of our entire history as a nation. We have been defined by it, have had our monarchs crowned in the light of it, have built our laws on the basis of it, have our most learned institutions steeped in it historically. The list could go on, but the message is clear – the whole warp and woof of our nation has been shaped, coloured and organized by the influence of Christianity.

Yet in many ways this is an historic thing. The life and vigour of this has gone. Christianity as a dynamic faith that changes life and brings meaning and sense to life has dried up for the vast majority. Christian history is behind us; it is not being imbibed or lived out by the vast majority of people today. This idea of being a nation living with a past history of Christianity, but having to all intents and purposes disowned it, is known as 'post-Christian'.

This notion has far-reaching implications in the way that we therefore conceive of the task of evangelism. 'Post-Christian' is neither Christian nor atheistic – that is, 'belief' in God still exists in most people, but it is very far from what the Universal Christ came to bring. Faith is understood, but not in a personal way that appropriates fully what God has revealed of himself in and through Jesus Christ. It is not that people's belief patterns are untouched by the gospel, but more that there has been a loss of ownership of the gospel, and more especially of the Church's proclamation of the gospel, and therefore by association with the Church itself as the guardian of the faith. In many ways this type of 'faith' can be more resistant to the gospel than the pre-Christian paganism which existed in previous generations.

However, this should be seen alongside another important element. Whilst the West may have become post-Christian, it has certainly not become secular, and whilst traditional religion may be in retreat, it has not been, in the current scheme of things, entirely replaced by rationalism. Traditional religion may be on the back burner, but we are far from secular. One only has to take a brief look at our modern societies to see that they are still replete with religions and spiritualities of every kind, both short-lived and longer-lasting.

This therefore leads us on to further analysis of being a post-Christian nation. Being 'post-Christian' is often labelled by us evangelicals as a bad thing – that is to say, we are a pagan people who have rejected our Christian heritage; we have disowned all that Christianity has brought to us, and now we are adrift, in need of conversion once again to being a Christian nation. Yet it is this negative view of the post-Christian scene that needs challenging if we are to realistically be an evangelistic influence in the current climate.

Off the starting-blocks

However we understand 'post-Christian', what cannot be denied is that millions of people in the Western world believe in God, and believe that he is with them in some way, and pray at times. They are probably uncomfortable about going into the details of their beliefs, but those beliefs are real for many people. In a recent survey, 55 per cent of the population said they still regard themselves as Christian, even though they may have almost totally disregarded the Church from their thinking or lifestyle. A poll in 1990 showed that 76 per cent believe in God, 69 per cent in sin, 60 per cent in heaven, 48 per cent in life after death. Another survey revealed that 47 per cent of the population in England, Scotland and Wales were notional Christians, and 8 per cent were nominal. Notional Christians are those who would identify themselves as Christian, but have never been churchgoers and would not identify themselves with any denomination. Nominal Christians are here defined as those who would identify themselves with a denomination or local church but may not have ever been regular or even occasional attendees. Their involvement may be through family, childhood or rites of passage.

These figures are representative of millions of people who have perhaps lost their way spiritually through very little fault of their own, but are still wanting to identify themselves as Christian, even though they do not want to identify themselves with the rigours of the Church again. They are not expressing this faith through organized religion, but it simmers gently away in their lives, often expressed in private and personal ways. Often real faith can be there, but it is crowded out by the busy-ness of life and becomes stagnant and infertile.

For those of us who are evangelicals, such nominal or notional Christianity can often be thought of as not being 'proper Christianity'; it can be seen as dead wood in the Church that needs either cutting off or converting. This was powerfully illustrated when I was running a church-based training pro-gramme for students who were on a discipleship course. My role was to assess the suitability of the churches to host this kind of training programme. On the application form it asked for an analysis of the church's growth situation. One particular church had experienced some growth and said, on the positive side, that it was 'a warm, friendly church', but on the negative side it said that the church was a good church for nominal Christians!

This was seen as a bad thing in that it was thought that there was obviously the lack of a cutting edge to the church, that allowed nominal Christians to stay that way. Yet this should be seen as a good thing, in that it means that people who are happy to explore at a basic, fringe level can be allowed to do so. To try to draw them in closer when they are not ready can mean that we lose them completely.

It is all too easy for those whose faith is alive and well to think that such a type of Christian faith is no faith at all, that nominal or notional Christianity is an insult to the very idea of what Christianity is about – that is, a personal and living relationship with God through faith in Christ, expressed through the fellowship of the body of Christ. In many ways this is true; Christianity is a living faith that needs to be expressed and re-expressed through active involvement in prayer, worship, Holy Communion, teaching and discipleship. But this should not blind us to the fact that the notional and nominal expressions of Christianity can be a valid part of being on a spiritual pilgrimage. Faith is not always expressed in the same way for everyone. Such faith may be enough to grow in the right circumstances and can be seen in a positive light. The nominal pilgrim should not necessarily be seen merely as a 'sinner who needs converting', but may in fact already be responding to as much of God as they know with as much of their self as they know.

In understanding the post-Christian scene as a rejection of the gospel and a hostility to the preaching of Christ, it can seem justifiable to think that people are pagan or heathen. But they may not in fact be quite so anti-Christian as we think; they may have been more influenced by the person of Christ in their thinking than we give them credit for. Mission in a post-Christian world means that we acknowledge this and give people credit for it. Christianity may not be a dynamic aspect of their lives, but it has helped to shape who they are, which may be more telling than how much of what we preach they accept.

Christian values

Another aspect of this is that not only have their beliefs been influenced by Christianity in a positive way, but their values have also. Many of the principles that people still hold to are based on Christian principles. We only have to read the newspapers and look around to see that many still hold beliefs that have been influenced by Christianity.

On one occasion as a minister I had to marry two couples in one day. The first marriage was for a couple who had been deeply involved and committed to the church for some years. Almost everyone at the wedding was either part of the congregation or was well familiar with what Christians said and thought. The second marriage was quite different. It was for a couple who had almost no contact with the church. Their entire family was unchurched and they themselves had expressed the early beginnings of faith only very recently, and deepened it in their marriage preparation. For this wedding almost no one in the church was Christian.

For the marriage where the majority were outside the Church, what I decided to do was take the content of the first marriage, which was thoroughly biblical, and take the Christian principles, but clothe them in an earthy garb, using chatty illustrations and only the occasional reference to the Bible. After the service many said they thought it was great, and their first time in church was a great experience. But I particularly remember one woman who came up to me and said she was not a church-goer but had been married for 50 years and was still together, and thought she was a good example to these young people and wanted them to do the same. This woman was undoubtedly influenced by Christian teaching on marriage and, from further discussion, I found out that she warmed to the life and teaching of Jesus in a more general way, even though she was not identifying with the Church as such.

Society as a whole is deeply influenced by Christ and his teaching. The Hebrew and Christian traditions of the Bible have acted as salt and light down through the centuries and have undoubtedly left their mark on how we live. These aspects of salt and light have provided a foundation for many of our institutions, and a basis on which to build our understanding of the way that a society should function at all levels. Centuries of Christian belief have shaped the way that we conduct our lives and run our society.

At the popular level, the aphorisms of Jesus and biblical sayings have thoroughly infested our culture: 'Love thy neighbour', 'Do unto others', 'The blind leading the blind', 'Blessed are the peacemakers', 'What you sow, you reap'. People may not realize that these quotes come from Jesus and the Bible, but the society in which we all live has been profoundly shaped by this ethos, and people may be standing on the very foundation that Jesus and the Church have built, without realizing it.

At the more political level, we see the general belief that those in power are there to serve the people and not their own ends. This idea of servant leadership has been influenced by the life and death of Jesus. He taught the world that he came to serve, which in some Western countries is expressed through the national life on Maundy Thursday, which reminds us of the time when Jesus washed his disciples' feet. We are disturbed when those in power abuse it and use it for their own ends. In the West, Christian teaching has served to illuminate the task of the national leaders. The gospel acts as salt and light and is still doing its work of purifying and enlightening.

In many ways this national presence of the Church and Christian heritage in the West can be likened to the deserted mansion that everybody knows is there but nobody goes to or lives in. Its presence is still there, and by virtue of that presence it exerts an influence. People know it is there and may refer to it when giving directions to someone asking the way, but they do not see it in a way that influences their lives. What needs to happen to that mansion is that the lights need to go on and it needs to be transformed into something that is relevant to the needs of the people who have previously only seen it as derelict. If people are suspicious as to why they are being invited to this once derelict mansion, they will not go, but if its activities are thought of as good and beneficial and without hidden agenda, they will go because they know how to get there. It may take time to overcome prejudices or suspicion, but eventually they enter its gates because all along they have been only too aware of its existence.

In view of all this, to see people as pilgrims helps us to avoid thinking that the gospel has only worked if we feel certain that they have fulfilled various unwritten criteria, and helps us to see it as something that is still working within our society and which stands over against our society and makes its claim upon it. It continues by its life to influence and shape the way that people and leaders think.

An individual gospel

One of the significant developments in Western society since the Enlightenment is that of individual emancipation. In times before the Enlightenment the community generally took priority over the individual (this is something of a generalization, as the individual was discussed at the philosophical level in ancient Greece), but after the Enlightenment the individual and his or her pursuit of happiness and fulfilment became paramount. Individuals became much more of a category in themselves; they could believe what they wanted, how they wanted; they could do as they chose without regard to society. The right of individual freedom became inviolable.

The evangelistic task in turn also placed an emphasis on the individual. We became focused on the need for an individual's decision. Numbers of conversions were counted in terms of individuals who raised their hands at meetings or who said a certain prayer. Dwight L. Moody (1837–99), the leading North American evangelist of the last quarter of the 19th Century, rose to fame in the heyday of individualism. He preached a message that viewed the sinner as standing alone before God. The Holy Spirit was understood primarily as working in the heart of individuals and known through personal experience. The response to Moody's preaching was thus one that each individual had to make. Such sayings as 'The Christianity that doesn't begin with the individual doesn't begin; the Christianity that ends with the individual ends' became maxims for what happens at conversion. This saying (which I remember being taught at Bible college), whilst redressing the individualistic first part with a communal second part, still defines becoming a Christian in individualistic terms. Such an understanding of conversion meant that the gospel was seen as succeeding only if individuals were converted in a fairly well-defined way.

Yet the notion of pilgrimage rightly raises some questions about this individualistic need for personal conversion. Is the end result of evangelism about individuals responding to the gospel in certain ways, or can we reconceive it as something that is also communal, corporate and part of a wider pilgrimage?

Whilst the redemption that Jesus provided has opened up the possibility for the individual to know peace with God, we should not lose sight of the fact that the gospel is good news to the whole of society and a communal good that affects those living under it. Many revivals historically took place in close-knit communities where it was the faith of the whole community that helped to carry the individual to faith – indeed, this is the message of 'whole households' in Acts (Acts 7:10; 16:33; cf. 2 Timothy 4:19). The whole household coming to faith was the New Testament writer's understanding of the way that the community worked; it expressed his world-view of life in those days. All in that household did not come to faith in the same sense, nor express their faith in the same way or with the same convictions, yet the author is happy to consider them as coming to faith because they were part of the communal faith in Christ that took place. In Hebrew thought there was an underlying ethos of corporate solidarity; the individual was always thought of in the collective (family, tribe, nation), and the collective in the individual.

With a more communal mind-set, we would approach individual conversion from a very different angle. Rather than starting with the individual person and then asking how this person can become a Christian, we would begin with the intrinsic interrelatedness of the person to the wider community or group, and then see how their individual response of faith, in the context of interrelatedness, can properly flourish.

The emphasis on the individual standing before God and the focus on individual conversion has meant that we evangelicals are in danger of perhaps losing sight of the communal, corporate nature of Christian faith. Taken to its extreme, individualism can end in a tragic isolationism.

An individual may not express their own beliefs and spirituality in the terms that we evangelists want, but this does not always mean that we should see them as unbelievers. Many of the values they already hold to are because of historic Christian belief and heritage (e.g. a belief in heaven, a general outlook of honesty, general acceptance of Christian morality, views of non-violence). Their adherence to the corporate values of a nation that still has Christian belief at its core, or even more intimate involvement with a Christian denomination or church, may in fact be a very significant building-block which we are not fully appreciating.

One family that I worked very closely with will always remind me of this. The husband and children were absolute pillars of the local church. They were at every meeting, would pray and worship their hearts out, and were full of enthusiasm for the Lord and his ways. This was not the case with the wife in the family, though. She almost never came to the church and did not accept the evangelical call for a personal conversion experience or to hand one's life over to the lordship of Jesus. She did, however, believe in God and the life of Jesus, and whilst she did not pray herself, she did believe in prayer. In fact, one time when one of the children was ill, the husband was talking about going to the doctor the next day when his wife said, 'Well, pray about it before you go to bed, and we'll see how she is in the morning.' It was almost as if she had more faith in prayer than he did. Yet this person, according to all the evangelicals she had met, was not a Christian because she did not match up to the evangelical criteria. Indeed, she had been told so many times that because she had never made a personal commitment and had never had any conversion experience, she was not a Christian, so she began to think that she wasn't, even though before she came into contact with Christians she had always thought of herself as a Christian, if only in a notional sense.

And yet the tremendous kindness she showed, and the generosity of spirit that she exhibited, and the acceptance that she showed to the faith of her family, said to me that faith can be more than an individual response. It was almost as if there was a family faith that she was part of. This is not to say that her relationship with God is as good as it could be; it is recognizing that she too has a faith that should not be seen as placing her outside of Christianity. She should be encouraged to keep on walking, because her walk with faith is a pilgrimage, which is a valid situation to be in, even when that pilgrimage is not leading directly to the doors of a church. It may end at the doors of the church, but it may not, and it may go by a very roundabout route to get there. Both of these should be accepted.

What to do with such a 'pick 'n' mix'

Julie had a good understanding and knowledge of the Bible for someone outside the Church. She also believed in the miracles of the Old and New Testaments and thought that Jesus was a good standard to live by. Once, whilst talking with some friends over coffee about personality traits that we all had, when one characteristic was identified that Julie had, she happened to say that she was like this because this was just like the animal that she was in the Chinese birth signs. This brought a reaction from another Christian present, who told her that this was not compatible with Christian belief and that the Bible condemned astrology of all sorts.

As we talked over sausage rolls and a glass of wine after the funeral service, one of the relatives of the deceased said that they were now 'looking down on us', enjoying our eating and drinking, as they were partial to a few drinks themselves and were probably having one with us in a far better place where it wasn't as expensive as their local! The relatives of the person who had died were not associated with the church, except one son, who was an active member and provided a Christian circle of friends for the family. Everyone outside the church laughed at this comment and thought it brought a good atmosphere to the occasion. Those inside the church let it go at that point, but several months later they brought this issue up again, saying that it is only God who can see what we are doing, not dead relatives, and that not everyone goes to heaven when they die – this is in God's hands, but it is not automatic entry.

Our 'pick 'n' mix' society means that there are few stock beliefs in people's lives. Each person makes up their own mind and thinks that they are right. Each situation and each person's beliefs are different; they pick and mix as they choose, combining Christian beliefs with all sorts of other beliefs, some half-Christian, some from other spiritualities. Since this is the case, we need to listen carefully to what people are saying and what their values and experiences are. If they are coming from a notional or nominal perspective of Christianity, then we need to be willing to encourage them in that, and not tell them that this is not proper Christianity, but through our own life and interaction help them to see what our faith means to us in the everyday stuff of life.

We are called to present truth, but the notion that pilgrimage is a valid state to be in means that we can do so without marginalizing the way that most people think whilst they are on this pilgrimage. The more they can identify with us, the more that, in time, they will reach their own conclusions and indeed be in a better relationship with God to sort these issues out for themselves. People's pick 'n' mix thoughts can be theologically inaccurate and should not necessarily be endorsed by the Church, but in both of the above stories it shows how much of people's thinking has been influenced by Christianity, and shows that seeds of faith are in these people's lives and need to be watered and nourished, not trampled on because they do not square up with the details of evangelical faith.

It is our responsibility in the evangelistic challenge, as the ones who want to communicate something to people, to understand the beliefs and way of life of those to whom we want to send the message. It is helpful to remember that one of the miracles of the Day of Pentecost was that each person was able to hear the message of salvation in their own language. We need, as those empowered by the same Spirit, to hear and understand the language, culture and mind-set of those from whom we seek a response.

This requires listening before speaking, living before acting, and empathizing before guiding.

Back on the pilgrim trail

It is with all this in mind that we return to the theme of pilgrimage. If pilgrims in our society are influenced by Christianity in an indirect way and have still retained some of the basic tenets of belief in their thinking, then sharing our faith with them must take this into consideration. People may be resistant and hardened to the *preaching* of the gospel, but may not be resistant to the *message* of the gospel. It may be that people are rejecting our preaching of the gospel without rejecting God.

We must relate to them as people who may well be *not yet* believers in the God of our Lord Jesus Christ who, for whatever reason, have rejected the clichés of evangelical faith but are ready to express faith in ways that are relevant to their everyday needs. They may not have had a conversion experience, but if the Church is to be in the market-place once more, we need to realize that people are on a journey and may be at the point of having travelled many miles, and in need of rest and restoration before they continue. They may have taken many wrong turns and may be slowly reorienting themselves.

Chapter 6

MADONNA, KABBALA AND THE NEW SPIRITUALITY

> There is not one square inch of the entire creation about which
> Jesus Christ does not cry out, 'This is mine! This belongs to me!'
>
> Abraham Kuyper

Scientists tell us that if the universe were not ordered and fashioned as it is, we would not be here to talk about it! If it were not for the great red stars, the supernovas, the galaxies and the planets, all of which are necessary to make life possible in all its complexity and splendour, we would not be able to exist. As Christians we believe that behind this wonderful and exhilarating creation lies a personal and loving God who made it all and continues to work throughout his entire creation to bring about his great and final purposes.

The Bible teaches us that God does not just intend to bring all humans to their fulfilment, but all of creation – indeed, the entire cosmos (Romans 8:20–22). All of creation, whilst itself groaning, is moving towards God's final purposes, eagerly awaiting its redemption. This does not arise from within the creation itself but because of the work of the Holy Spirit, who is redeeming all of creation according to the final plans of him who created all things. Just as the Spirit of God once hovered over an empty and void creation, so he ever continues to be present from above and from within, working throughout the entire fabric of creation to bring all into subjection to the lordship of Jesus. If we truly believe that it is his sovereign work to redeem fallen people and cause God's goodness to be seen and experienced among humankind, then we must also accept that his gracious activity is taking place all over the world and creating opportunities in every event. He is working to redeem each and every situation. Our task is to find out what he is doing in each situation and to join in.

Yet this redemptive activity of God extends to all the trends and movements within the whole of creation, or the cosmos, as it is now referred to. The increased and almost phenomenal growth of interest in spirituality must be considered part of this. To this we now turn.

Shocking, amazing!

God has since the beginning been revealing himself as the Lord of all the nations, whose purpose is universal and whose work in the world has always been far bigger than we have believed. Right through the Bible we have many 'shock factors' that challenge our limited horizons and encourage us to think of God's work of redemption in much broader terms than we have done previously. These messages of broadening horizons are needed today in evangelicalism, where there has been a tendency to limit the work of God to our own understanding, and to forget that God's outreach is universal in its scope and unlimited in its intent. As soon as we take away this universal aspect from the character and work of God, we start to see only what we want to see and see only as far as our own limited horizons. God's horizons are limitless, and he calls us to be like him.

From very early on in God's self-revelation to his people, he provides various 'set pieces' that encourage them to think outside their boundaries. There is the story of Balaam in Numbers 22–24, which is the only one from antiquity to present him in a positive light. Yet here we find something quite startling – that he is actually used by God to pronounce blessing on Israel, confesses Yahweh as his God, and the Spirit of God comes upon him. Balaam was hardly a model believer, but we find in fact that God was able not only to endow a dumb animal with human speech, but also to cause a pagan diviner to speak of divine things.

For Rahab, a prostitute outside the community of Israel, the only way her faith could possibly be expressed was to tie a ribbon around a window and tell a little white lie (Joshua 2:5, 18). Yet this act of obedience and defiance distinguished her from everyone else as a believer. The New Testament writer of the Book of Hebrews even considers her actions as counting her among the heroes of faith (Hebrews 11:31).

In Isaiah 45 we have Cyrus, the king of a heathen nation, being used by God and called his 'anointed'. It is through Cyrus that God will do his work. This no doubt came as a great surprise to the Hebrews, who thought that God only worked through their own little nation. This message is repeated again and again, nowhere more starkly than in Amos 9:7, where God, who goes to great lengths to reveal himself to Israel and to emphasize their place as his covenant people, also reveals that he has been working among other nations: 'People of Israel, I think as much of the people of Sudan as I do of you. I brought the Philistines from Crete and the Syrians from Kir, just as I brought you from Egypt.' It seems that God is saying that each of these nations has had its own exodus experience.

In the New Testament we find three non-Hebrew women mentioned anonymously as part of the ancestry of Jesus (Matthew 1:3, 5–6). We find Jesus himself saying that the faith of a Gentile soldier was as great as that of the Patriarchs. We see pagan magicians worshipping at the feet of the baby Jesus, and the dislocated and disenchanted of society eagerly accepted by God, while the religious leaders find no place.

Rahab, Uriah, Ruth, Balaam and the numerous New Testament characters all teach us to listen to God's voice beyond the edges of our comfort zone. These shock factors startle us as we realize that orthodox confessions of faith are found on the most unlikely lips.

Christianity works because it is true and is the way that God has chosen to supremely reveal himself as the Creator-Redeemer whose way of salvation is the way of costly personal identification. It is the way of passion, suffering love, death and resurrection. To the fractured story of humanity, whose life is one of alienation, separation from God and struggle to emerge into all the potential that has been given to it, this suffering love is good news. To those who accept this according to God's revelation of himself, there is much joy, but to those who still grasp at the truth and see it dimly, there yet remain the seeds of hope. Just because God has made this revelation clear to some does not mean to say that those who have not accepted this message as fully as we have remain outside of God's grace and blessing. Perhaps such people are even raised up by God when we become parochially minded to remind us that it is God's mission to redeem all people everywhere (2 Peter 3:9) and that he will do this despite us and beyond us. Such shocks remind us of the generosity and universality of God and goad us to be a bit more generous to others in our attitudes. Such an attitude of generosity will actually make us more winsome in people's eyes and therefore far better at demonstrating the purposes of God.

Spirituality is back on the agenda

Many people are beginning to put spiritual things back on their agenda, and the materialism of even a decade or so ago, whilst certainly still a powerful force, is by no means the only player on the field of themes in society. All around us we see an increased awareness of and interest in the spiritual dimensions of life. There is even a popular willingness to provide spiritual answers to things that have previously merely been accounted for scientifically or rationally. People want to talk about spiritual experiences, and it is now very acceptable to believe in some modern spiritual idea, ranging from horoscopes to Tai-Chi, from Feng

Shui to Karma. We find that many celebrities have openly identified themselves with spiritual beliefs of one sort or another. We have New Age books that have made it into the best-seller lists, along with books on a whole range of other spiritualities, from popular personality profiling in shamanism to more nature-oriented spiritualities (e.g. Gaia, alternative and holistic medicine, and crop circles), along with a whole array of spiritual and other-worldly card- and board-games.

Yet how is the Church seen in all this, and more importantly, how do we respond?

Whilst the emergence of a new spirituality is surely underway, a similar interest is not really being found in the traditional religions, especially Christianity, which is seen as part of the institutionalized structure that helped to create the mess we are now in. Christianity is perceived as of the 'old order' not the new, and is therefore to be discarded rather than trusted for the future. So how do we respond to this? Do we become negative and see the tide going against us, or do we think that this emergence of interest in spiritual things can be a good thing for the Church, if we learn how to set our sails right and pick up on this trend in society? Surely we are called to be a voice that works for reorientation from within the situation, rather than a noise from outside that people can walk away from. If we just stand on the street corners and shout out our message, people can turn that corner and walk away, which is what they have done. If we walk with them as they shop, we can be a voice that stays with them as they choose.

Recovering the radical

To properly develop a biblical approach to evangelism that is able to engage with the present trends in spirituality, we need to tread carefully and thoroughly.

Jesus was a radical. His life and teaching were at the cutting edge socially, politically, spiritually and theologically. We often think the word 'radical' means 'popular' and 'in with the in crowd'. But being a radical, by its very nature, means that we are constantly on the edge, moving other people in our direction. Being radical is not popular, as we see in the life of Jesus.

The teaching of Jesus about the Kingdom of God was radical in a way all by itself. We can sometimes mistakenly think that 'radical' means singing the most trendy worship choruses and having the latest high-tech gadgets. Or perhaps in some circles it is seen as having an approach to prayer that is dynamic and combatant against forces of darkness, or moving in the Spirit so that the gifts are exercised to a high and regular degree. And yet Jesus' demonstration of the radical Kingdom was his willingness to live a sacrificial life for those around him who were lost and broken. His radical lifestyle was one of loving and accepting every human being, especially those rejected by our religious systems; of redefining the boundaries, of taking risks at cost to his own reputation and standing. It meant living with people in the grey areas, because in so doing he ended up risking something of his own piety.

Walking in the wrong direction

Evangelism is often seen as taking people from where they are, grabbing them and turning them in the direction that we want them to go in, all too often with little care for the validity of their own experience. Yet in the story of Jesus on the road to Emmaus with the two disciples, a very startling picture of something quite different can be seen. Jesus, in his evangelistic ministry to these two disciples, was willing to walk with them in the wrong direction. They were walking away from Jerusalem, when he had told his disciples to wait in Jerusalem; they were in this regard going in the wrong direction. But it was only in his willingness to walk with them in the wrong direction that they recognized who he was. It was only by identifying with them, even in their mistakenness, that they in the end came to know him.

Radical evangelism, quite distinct from always making people conform, may also mean walking with people in the wrong direction, as Jesus did.

If such a trend of interest in spiritual things is fast becoming a theme in society, then we, the evangelical Church, need to be right there with it, building our own values into it and seeing each situation as something that contains the potential to lead this person towards Christ, rather than an aberration, a deviation that leads them to the devil.

A starting-place

To do this we need to recognize that people are spiritual beings. God created us this way, and the search for spirituality is a good thing that comes from God. Once we acknowledge this, we can see that when God starts to touch people in this non-material, spiritual side of life, he does so in a way that starts where they are at as people. Once we recognize that people's starting-places are not in themselves bad or necessarily wrong, we can learn to walk with them. Unfortunately, what has happened is that because people's starting-places have not been as 'Christian' as we would have liked, we have seen this form of spiritual expression as wrong and needing to be squashed or else avoided completely, in case it should develop and become even more aberrant.

One Christian friend of mine has workmates who are into tarot cards and even contacting the dead. When he told them that he did not agree with these expressions of spirituality, they didn't take too much notice and just carried on regardless. My friend decided that since they were obviously not going to change their views, he would just switch off whenever this subject was discussed and avoid the issue altogether. Yet such an approach is not going to be a constructive, non-confrontational voice in their experiences. To switch off because we do not agree and have not had an instant conversion only serves the purpose of writing ourselves out of the discussion. What we should be doing is encouraging others in their quest for spiritual expression in such a way that we can dialogue and discuss with people so that we can share with them our own Christian spirituality as they proceed along their way.

This does not mean that every form of spiritual expression in someone's life should be endorsed or encouraged by us. There are some aspects of spiritual exploration that can be harmful. What it does mean, however, is that we recognize that for the majority of people in the West at this time, the kind of beliefs that people are beginning to hold are legitimate starting-places that we should recognize as such. We should be prepared, in an attitude of respect and mutuality, to walk with them in this experience, without feeling the need to instantly convert them to an evangelical faith, since to do so may well nip their exploration in the bud, or else put them off getting closer to us further down the road.

And the rock was Christ

If we see all spirituality outside evangelical Christianity as corrupt, then we will hardly feel comfortable helping people in an exploration of this spirituality. Yet spirituality is a person's relationship with their everyday life and the sacred. Spirituality is the way we live in relationship to the sacred or the divine – the sense that we make of our lives in connection to the spiritual, numinous experiences that we have, or our beliefs about God. Events in our own life will shape our spirituality which, in turn, will affect the way we make sense of the world in which we live and the issues of life that confront us.

In 1 Corinthians 10 we have a remarkable statement that says simply that when the ancient Hebrew people where strengthened and succoured spiritually, whilst they did not know it, this strength was Christ. The rock which was their spiritual food and drink is identified as Christ. The text reminds us that Christ was spiritual nourishment before he was known or believed in. Whilst this is a biblical story concerning the community of God, should we see people today as so different? Christ can be people's spiritual nourishment even when he is not believed in, since he is the way to God, whether people know it or not.

Do you believe in ghosts?

A situation that illustrated to me how important it is to walk with people in the wrong direction rather than trying to instantly redirect them was to do with some people that I once worked with. My faith was something of an oddity to them, but they did try on several occasions to show some interest in this aspect of my life. On one occasion someone brought in a photo that they had taken which, for some reason I don't understand, exhibited a very strong image on it that looked like the ghostly shadow of someone. All the people that were meant to be in the photo were accounted for, except this one shadow of a person that the man who had taken the photo knew nothing about. Of course, it was something of a joke to some of the people there, and most treated it fairly light-heartedly, but their curiosity was aroused, and they wanted to enter into a playful discussion on whether there really was a ghost in this picture and, of course, whether ghosts actually existed. From here it moved on to communicating with the dead, as someone had a friend who had some experience of spiritualism, and on to other forms of spiritual activity.

My reaction to the ghost, although essentially light-hearted, was to pour cold water on the idea and to suggest that it was more appropriate to have faith in God than in ghosts, be they good ones or bad ones. At this time I saw spiritualism as the very pattern of evil, the very work of Satan himself, so I decided to condemn in stark terms this type of spirituality, which was forbidden in the Bible and which I saw as feeding a load of lies to the vulnerable.

Whilst what I was saying was probably generally the party line on such issues within the evangelical community, what happened was that what I said was so far removed from anything that anyone else could relate to or understand that they came to see what I believed about spiritual things as irrelevant to their own questions or concerns. After this occasion they never raised the issue of spiritual things again in my presence. I had rejected the interest that they had shown in spiritual things because it was so far removed from where I was and where I thought they should be. The result was that I burned the very bridges that they were trying to build – bridges that I would have cherished so dearly later on in those relationships.

In saying these things I did not realize that I may have been extinguishing the little faith that they did have and demolishing their starting-place. It also made light of the little bit of comfort that the bereaved family and friends of this person had found. It was wrong of me to expect people to disown what they had found to be beneficial, just because I thought it was wrong and ungodly. I should have established credibility in their eyes first and shown compassion to them and accepted that this was only a starting-place rather than the finishing-place.

I reacted in this way in this situation because I saw expressions of spirituality that did not shape up to my evangelical agenda as being something to be squashed in case they developed and led people astray. I would not allow people to explore their spirituality in any way that was not strictly evangelical or recognized as Christian.

Having learned this lesson, things took a very different turn when I was some years later presented with a not dissimilar situation. Some people I knew had become interested in 'dowsing' (the movement of a pendulum-type object to decide between one thing or another) and tarot cards, and had decided to try them out. For some of these people it seemed to be a matter of genuine curiosity, but one person in particular had some big decisions to make, and was seeking all the help he could get.

As I talked to this person, having learned something from my previous mistakes, I did not decry what he was doing and listened with interest as he told me that he did believe in the spiritual realm and felt that he needed some kind of supernatural help with his decisions. In his searching he had heard that dowsing worked because there was an energy in the universe and in people that could direct this pendulum to help them to make the right decisions, if they could somehow tap into these energies. As we talked this idea over in the weeks that followed, I always showed an interest in him, never told him that what he was doing was wrong, and told him that I too believed that there was a spiritual world alongside our material world. On one occasion I said that, when I had decisions to make, I prayed to God, who, for me, is a personal being who has a personal plan for my life, and indeed for all his people. This idea was very appealing to this person, who was touched by what I said.

I would love to be able to say he became a Christian there and then, but he didn't. I have long since lost contact with him, but he did mention to me once as we passed in the corridor that he had prayed about his situation a few days earlier. This was all he said, and then he walked off into the distance. I never spoke to him about it again and it never came up again, and shortly afterwards we went our separate ways.

It may not seem much, but to me it meant a great deal, because I know that this person was encouraged to step just one little bit closer to the God whom I know as a personal, loving Creator who directs his children personally to be involved in his own great purposes through a wonderful two-way communication system called prayer. And, of course, we can pray for such people ourselves, or in some cases pray with them. I have often been surprised, after establishing such a rapport with someone, how keen they are for me to pray a simple prayer with them. And, of course, such prayers form part of the overarching work of God himself. It would be very arrogant of me to think that God's involvement with this person stopped with me. My prayers may simply connect and co-operate with other things that God is doing in his life.

One of the keys to the future of evangelism is the way we handle 'searchers' such as this, who have probably not thought through all the implications of what they are doing and why, but can be helped by us to do just that and to make more sense out of their world than they previously have done. Such a capacity to walk with a broader range of spiritual expression will mean acknowledging that God's call on people's lives may begin in a very 'non-Christian' way but can lead to an expression of faith that looks more like the revelation handed down to us.

Theme tunes

What has been said so far operates very much at the personal level – that is, how we respond to individuals who are open to other forms of spirituality. What about the movements themselves, though – what about the ethos, ideas and values of the systems – how do we respond to these?

In many ways, what is true of the individual is true of the movement. We should not agree with everything that every belief espouses. There is much in these belief systems that is based on selfish pleasure-seeking, greed, pride and the suppression of people. A quest for meaning and spiritual identity that is rooted in the self at the expense of others should be shown for what it is, with our responsibility as Christians fully turned to speaking out for issues of equality and justice. Christianity is a faith that is rooted in the selfless life and death of One who gave himself in sacrifice. He came to give his life, not only in his life but also in his death. If we are not able to suggest to people that sacrifice and giving for the good of others, sometimes at personal expense, should be included in their spirituality, then we have done less than we should.

Yet this does not necessarily mean that the whole New Age movement is corrupt. Christianity itself does not have a blameless past when it comes to using spiritual themes for its own selfish purposes. It can seem at times that much evangelical communication sees other expressions of spirituality as corrupt and harmful. However, whilst certain spiritualities can be destructive to people, they surely have to be assessed on their merits, not just because they are not orthodox Christianity.

What we need is discernment and wisdom to be able to identify what is really going on in the movements and what it is in them that is good and what it is that is harmful, rather than just writing them off as of the devil. For example, religious cults or spiritualities and practices that dehumanize and devalue can often be identified as an evil incursion into what may be a genuine quest for spiritual identity. Alternatively, spiritualities that attempt to redress harmful practices should not necessarily be seen in this way.

For example, beliefs that claim direct revelation from God and that tend towards exclusivism and end up marginalizing and manipulating people should be identified as such by the Church. But on the other hand, some popular practices – such as the one in Native Indian Spirituality in North America, where people go out to the Camps and get buried alive, with only their head showing, in order to get in touch with nature – may seem ridiculous to us as Christians and could appear to the secular mind as completely off the wall, but they are not necessarily evil in themselves. Native Indian Spirituality is extremely popular with many people at this time, and the emphasis on the connectedness of the whole of creation and humankind with nature is to be welcomed. Humanity has exploited and abused creation, and it is a good thing if spiritualities redress this balance. It is helpful for us to remind ourselves here that faith, when deadened by the secular world, does not necessarily end in atheism, but often in spirituality; and this may be the first faltering steps of a quest in this spirituality that can lead on to a fuller encounter with God.

Then there is all the popular New Age literature such as *The Celestine Prophecy*, which was a best-seller in America and Britain. Much in this novel is good and helpful, and points to the need for a greater harmony between humans and creation, and between humans and humans. The solution that the book offers is that we can get our energy not through dominating and destroying each other but through a harmony with the universe. This idea of reconnecting with the natural world can be affirmed by Christians. But we can also add our own vision to it as well. Whilst elements of this book can be praised, we can also see that this idea alone is impersonal, and here Christians can speak of a Creator who is present throughout his universe in an intensely personal way. The oneness of humans with creation is not an end in itself but a means to knowing the One who created all this for his own purpose, so that the crown of his creation –

humankind itself – could come to a fuller and more complete co-operation with him who is Lord of all, Christ the Lord.

Then there is the emergence of a spirituality that attempts to combine spirituality and sexuality, perhaps most popularly expressed by Madonna. Christianity itself has not done a great job of addressing the spirituality of sexuality – in fact much of our history has been to do with the denial and suppression of sexuality. The early Church heavily emphasized the dichotomy between the body and the soul. Madonna herself had a strict Catholic upbringing that seemed to suppress sexual understanding, and some of the images she has sent out have been to do with throwing off a repressive view of sexuality associated with the Church. We only have to take note of the Church's reaction to her video 'Like a Prayer', which combines elements of sexuality and religion, to see that we are still uncomfortable about linking the two. Madonna's use of religious icons such as crosses, the stigmata and her name itself have also caused not a little disquiet in the Christian community. Whilst we would still want to criticize some of the framework in which this association of sexuality and spirituality is set, what makes Madonna especially worthy of note in this regard is that she is a gauge of our times. The current social anxieties and trends can often be observed in what Madonna has expressed. Her relocation of religious icons within celebrations of sexuality may signify that an appetite for an inner spiritual journey is awakening. The use of sexually electrified images can provide a spark to those who sense the need to take seriously self-knowledge and an inner awareness of spiritual identity.

Sexuality is an intensely personal and, indeed, spiritual element of our lives, and intercourse can be an intimate means of self-discovery, since we find ourselves most truly in our relationships with other persons. In many ways sex would perhaps be more wholesome, personal, intimate, passionate and transformative, in a world which has depersonalized, cheapened and trivialized it, if we could recapture a vision of divine *eros* – God's own passion for connection – as intrinsic to God's being.

If there is any area of authentic human existence that can be distorted, it is sex. This means that it is even more important that we enter the discussion in a way that enables us to realistically be part of it. If a movement, even in its formative days, is reaching out to make a connection between sexuality and spirituality, albeit marred, should we dismiss it out of hand because it gets expressed in ways that are not strictly the best? To dismiss as 'wrong' or 'sinful' something that is undoubtedly connecting with many people, for whatever reason, without trying to understand why this is so and make sense out of it in the light of developments in Christian thought, means that we can write ourselves out of the discussion. The West, for example, could perhaps learn much from Eastern practices in Tantric sex, which stresses the interface between sexuality and spirituality – that sex can be a magical and mystical experience. Sex has the power to convey deep feelings of pleasure and loss, the potential to further one's spiritual being, and to encounter one's partner not in a cheapened form of casual sex but sacramentally and wholly. Such truths can inform views of sex that are either too casual or too restrictive.

What is true of such modern spiritual trends is true of most nascent movements. Even in many Christian movements it can take time to find balance and a way through. To react against these movements without recognizing that they may express some truth will only mean that we dismiss something that for millions makes some sort of sense. It also means that we run the risk that they will give little credence to the constructive criticism that we do make, not only to them as individuals but also to the movement, because we have now become known as those who are opposed to it lock, stock and barrel.

These are just some examples I have chosen to demonstrate that evangelism must be about more than just trying to convert people to Christianity, no matter where they start from, in one fell move. It must be about being a voice that speaks into the spiritualities that are present in our time, whilst endeavouring to build our own values into them so that people will not have to travel such a distance when they do move closer to God through Christ, because they will have already received some of what we stand for in the belief or spirituality that started them moving.

Highways

Whatever the reader may make of this, what cannot be denied is that this is the world in which people are now living. Society is full of other spiritual movements. These are the other voices that people will be hearing. Whatever they hear us say, they will be hearing it not as an isolated call from God but through the filter of all the other voices out there as well. It is in this environment of multiple-nascent spiritualities that we become just one more belief system. An evangelistic proclamation that calls people to join us because we are in the truth and everyone else is in error may not cut it any more, but an evangelistic proclamation that speaks into the other spiritualities and into the lives of the people themselves may become the voice of Christ on the Emmaus road. When people do embrace other forms of spirituality, this should not be seen as the road to hell, but a path whose route is not fixed – a sort of *Back to the Future* highway, where the conclusion remains open.

And if this is so, then it would be far better if this openness had within it the clear and distinctive voice of the Church, beckoning all to a fuller realization of God's purposes as revealed in Jesus Christ. The pilgrim may walk through many different places before arriving at his or her final resting place, and it is far better to be known in part by them than not at all, and better still to have helped them on their way through involvement, identification, relationship and respect, rather than hindering them because they have not taken the route that we thought they should.

Chapter 7

IN MEMORY OF FREDDIE MERCURY

Sin kills by perverting, polluting and dividing, breaking down persons and their vital relationships.

Cornelius Plantinga Jr

Tim was sitting on the steps that led up to Peter and Judy's flat, situated right on the seafront of Hove esplanade. He had been waiting there for some time, as he desperately wanted to talk to us about his life, his faith and his sexual orientation.

Tim wanted to make a faith commitment to the Lord Jesus. He was a homosexual, had always been one and enjoyed being one. He was not promiscuous and, like so many homosexuals living within the gay community, he gained a great deal of his identity and lifestyle from this community.

He had been linked to us for some weeks, having first come across our church when staying in an hotel where one of the members of our church was also a resident. As we explained to him what coming to faith and trust in Jesus was all about and the need for repentance and faith, he asked us about his homosexuality. We talked this issue through with him, saying that this was for God to deal with, but that homosexual practice was incompatible with God's will and would be something that in time he would need to address if he was to walk in the will and purpose of God. I remember Tim's reaction when we told him this. It was one of perplexity, hurt and confusion, all rolled into one. It was like we were insulting him in a way that, at the time, I just could not understand. It was almost as if we were saying that he could no longer be Tim; he had to become someone else. Tim was so hurt by our comments that he resorted to shock tactics and explained in graphic detail why he expressed his sexuality in the way he did. We talked, we discussed, but Tim was deeply, deeply wounded by what he had heard.

When he walked away from that conversation, we thought that in time God would break through and change his heart. He was never to be seen or heard of again.

Evangelism as reflection

If evangelism is to be about more than just winning people to our cause and converting them into church attendees, then an important aspect of evangelism is to reflect the values and life of the Kingdom of God back into society. If broadcasters tell us that one of their roles is to reflect back society to itself, then one of the roles of the Church is to reflect back the face of Christ into society. The Church in this regard becomes an evangelistic icon of the Kingdom to a society that is in need of the light, love and hope of Christ.

The Church is a community of pilgrims who have been bound to God in a covenant relationship and called by him to communicate to the wider world a foretaste of the salvation that is available to all and can touch all. The Church as the body of Christ, called to go where Christ would go and to say what Christ would say, is called to be a visible and effective sign of the transformational power of God that is made possible through integration into and involvement with this body, which in turn can have a transforming effect on society itself.

The evangelistic mission in this regard does not merely look after its own interests, it does not just concern itself with increasing its own numbers, for to do so reduces its mission to a particular sphere of interest, which will result in a fellowship that is unable to grasp the challenges of the society of which we are a part. Instead of pursuing a narrow spirituality, the Church is called to be a model for all humanity to see – a community that manifests faith, hope and love, qualities which reflect the being and character of the God whom we worship. In this sense the Church is called to offer more than a 'social gospel', but to point to a new pattern of reality in response to God's purpose of renewing all of creation (Romans 8:21).

The Church can become such a believable sign of salvation to the world when it displays to humanity a shadow of God's immi- nent reign – a Kingdom of reconciliation, peace and new life. Evangelism in this sense then becomes not merely an issue of win- ning people by inclusion, but of winning them by persuading them that the values that we live by are values that are worth living by for all people, and are necessary for a world that needs to be at peace with itself. It is not so much about saying we are right and you are wrong, but of sharing the reflection of Christ with the society that we are a part of, whereby people become challenged and changed by living under the piercing light of a Church that has itself learned to be the reflection of the glory of Christ.

This is being a Church that is cultural but also counter- cultural. Cultural in that we share in the struggle that humanity itself goes through, but counter-cultural in that we reflect back into society's brokenness the wholeness of Christ.

This chapter is about homosexuality, and it is in this area that the Church in its mission to the world can be a sign and fore- taste of God's imminent Kingdom. Whatever we may feel about the rights and wrongs of homosexual behaviour, what is appar- ent is that homosexuals experience prejudice and injustice in society. Whilst there now exists in society a relative comfort with gay sex, this can be superficial, and sometimes the willingness to treat gays as fully equal is dependent on whether they make their gayness invisible. This is so apparent to some homosexual Christians who have written on the social and political issues of homosexuality that they recommend that the gay person should 'blend in' with a heterosexual society, that they should effectively 'pass' on being homosexual so that they can accrue the social and economic advantages that similar heterosexuals do. A hierarchical, patriarchal, capitalist society can foster an environment of economic power and control that can become a basis for oppression to those who do not seem to fit. Sexism, racism, homophobia, classism, ableism and ageism all have the same origin, an origin where those who are either different to or weaker than the majority are excluded.

Society itself has its own patterns of social and cultural life that are so pervasive that this 'difference' means that those who do not seem to fit become marginalized. Sameness is prized and difference is shunned. I have read only recently of a black lesbian woman who was a Christian but who, in coming to terms with her sexuality, felt that she was on the fringes of an already marginalized urban black community. She was an ignored sexual outsider who nobody seemed to understand.

Regardless of what we think about the right or wrong of homosexual practice, gays are fellow human beings who are made in the image of God and deserve to be treated with the same dignity, equality and respect that the majority are treated with. In the light of this, questions about sexuality can be understood as more than simply personal matters, but are to do with deeper issues of social justice.

Some of the major church denominations have recently produced documents on homosexual behaviour, and many of them have focused on this social aspect of homosexuality and the false privileging of heterosexuality and the promotion of male dominance. The biblical authority on the subject of homosexuality, rather than located solely in the moral framework, sees the Gospels as telling the story of Jesus, which points to God's extensive love for all, that calls us to correct sins of status that exclude people. The Jesus story is one of emancipation in that it forms a community that reaches towards the new Kingdom of God where racial, ethnic, status and gender boundaries no longer exist (Galatians 3:28). This shift helps us to see that homosexuality is not merely about moral purity but about inclusion, justice, love, social oppression, wholeness and self-fulfilment. The exclusion of gays and lesbians from the full life of the Church is therefore seen to be sinful. This too has profound implications for those who believe that homosexual behaviour is always and necessarily sinful. Christians who believe this need to ask themselves whether it is right to place their interpretative emphasis on purity concerns, which means that they will feel qualified in continuing to see practising homosexuals as immoral outsiders, or alternatively on the constant 'love of neighbour' (Matthew 5:43; Romans 13:9; James 2:8) and 'hospitality to the stranger' (Matthew 25:35) teaching of the New Testament, which means that they would be willing to let go of these other concerns for the appropriation of a greater, more prevalent teaching in the Bible.

The greater wrong we did to Tim was not that we moralized about his homosexuality, but that we denied him the full and equal rights of entry to the Kingdom and the Church because of it.

If homosexuality is about more than issues of moral purity and becomes an issue of social justice, then it impinges on the mission of the Christian community. It is our task not only to bring acceptance and inclusion to the homosexual but also to reflect back to society the equality of the Kingdom of God where there is injustice. By including the homosexual and by giving full equality to homosexuals in the same way as is shown to heterosexuals, we reflect the justice-love of God back into our own prejudices, into those of other people, and into society itself. This way we actually constitute a change in society, since our values then become a touchstone to society's boundaries of exclusion.

Shock tactics again

If homosexuals are on the fringes of the Church and indeed society, then it would be quite in accord with the teaching of the New Testament that they can teach us something of great value.

Jesus often used those on the fringes to bring home a startling truth to those who excluded them from society. The Samaritans are used by Jesus to demonstrate true love and true religion (Luke 10:25–37), the poor are used to illustrate the riches of relationship with God (Matthew 5:3), a tax gatherer is used to demonstrate the transforming power of Christ in the lives of the repentant and humble (Luke 19:4), and a reprobate son is used to say that the rebels in society (e.g. prostitutes, tax collectors) can attain a closeness to the Father that the religious leaders of the day deny themselves because of their hubris (Luke 15:11–32). Yet, most startling of all, perhaps, for our purposes in this chapter is Jesus' use of a sexually immoral woman (Luke 7:44–49) and a eunuch to show that the morally despised can express something of what it means to be a true disciple, even if it wasn't appreciated at the time (Matthew 19:12).

The story of the immoral woman in Luke is used to highlight the purity of devotion to the Lord Jesus that came from someone who was despised because of her sexual reputation, but which was denied to Jesus by someone who should have really shown it. The point of the story was really that the very social customs of the day – giving water for the feet, giving a kiss and anointing the head with oil – were the very things that the host should have given to Jesus but didn't. By this token the denial of these things was itself a massive insult and social humiliation, and it was these very things that the 'immoral woman' did because of her love for the Lord, and because she was herself so hurt and dismayed that the One she had come to love should be so publicly humiliated at this meeting.

Jesus extends the hand of acceptance and forgiveness to someone who was excluded because of the attitudes of those who should have known better. This tells us that worse than her sexual sins were those of status-marking, boundary erecting and other-dominating. These sins, which had become socially acceptable (see vv. 42–43), became the very ones highlighted by Jesus. The irony of the story, of course, is not that sins can be calculated but that when we come to a realization of how great our sin is, we love the Lord even more.

If this story tells us that Jesus highlights the social exclusion policies of the day and turns them on their head by himself suffering humiliation, and extending the hand of acceptance to someone excluded by such social and moral demarcations, then the saying about the eunuch takes us one step further.

In the Old Testament eunuchs were excluded from the assembly of Yahweh (Deuteronomy 23:1; cf. Isaiah 56:4–5) and were alien to Jewish culture. Whilst they were given status in some Eastern courts, this was not true of them within the national life of Israel in the Old Testament or in the time of Jesus. So the idea here introduced by Jesus of making oneself a eunuch for the sake of the Kingdom would have been loathsome to Jewish minds. It would have been shocking to Jesus' hearers to think that those who had been impotent from birth or who were voluntarily castrated could be so for the sake of the Kingdom of heaven. Jesus was wanting to draw attention to a despised minority group to make a point, just as he used other people and groups to do the same thing. So what was Jesus' point?

The point was that those who were sexually outside of the community of Israel through no fault of their own, who were even shunned because of it, could not only be included in the Kingdom of heaven, but their condition was one that could be voluntarily entered into for the very sake of the Kingdom. This may well be the very reason that Luke tells us about the Ethiopian eunuch in Acts 8:26–40, as in his purpose of breaking down the preconceived ideas of where and how the good news of Jesus could be accepted, he decided to really shake his readers up and extend this to a foreigner who also happened to be a sexual outsider. A eunuch may have been excluded from the assembly of Yahweh in the Old Testament, but he is welcomed in the assembly of the Messiah in the New Testament.

What cannot be denied is that this saying of Jesus has certainly been the one that has given single people (also 'outsiders' in Jesus' time) a dignity and place previously denied them, and it may well be that the principle behind this saying should now be extended to homosexuals also. If homosexuals are sexual outsiders who still suffer socially from prejudicial attitudes and have been shunned because of their sexual orientation, then it is now time to give them a respect and dignity by welcoming them into the community of the Church as functioning members of the body of Christ. Jesus' use of the eunuch may even prompt us to think that the sexually despised can actually teach us something.

Many may feel that homosexual activity can never be tolerated and allowed for in the Church. Yet the Church is in the middle of the homosexual debate, the arguments are mooted and other areas of study and academic pursuit are informing our understanding of the Bible's comment, which still remains, however, the ultimate authoritative source on the subject. Developments in biology and psychology – areas of study that the Church has accepted in other fields – have taught us much about the nature of human sexuality, and it is necessary to understand homosexuality within this larger frame of reference. It is not being any more 'biblical' to deny or ignore what these disciplines have to teach us than it is to allow such knowledge to inform our understanding of the big themes that run through the Bible.

As has been mentioned, the themes of love for neighbour and justice for the stranger (justice-love) are incredibly weighty themes that run through the entire Bible. These incidents in the life of Jesus recounted above are high points, of course, but the theme of God's love and acceptance extending to all sinful people begins right at the start of the Bible. The notion that all people, even sinful ones, should be allowed justice and equality is equally abundant. What we have to ask ourselves, then, is whether the sinfulness of a homosexual relationship is a theme of equal weight to that of justice-love. If we were to put the theme of justice-love on one side of the scales and the sinfulness of a homosexual relationship on the other, which side would tip the balance? If you think that the sinfulness of homosexuality outweighs the need to demonstrate justice and love to those whose sins are greater than our own, then this chapter has nothing more to say to you. If you think that the issue of justice-love is a bigger issue, then that requires that you think more about this.

If we feel that we can continue to disallow homosexuals a place in our churches on the basis that this is more sinful and repulsive to God than accepting them is loving and just, then we may be doing so at the very great cost of marginalizing a whole people group.

Finding a place

When Jennifer found out that her boyfriend Gary was a homosexual, it tore her apart. It just didn't seem to make any sense. They had been going out together for two years, and yes, there had been some difficulties, but on the whole everything seemed so normal, so right.

The situation for Gary was very different. He was in his midtwenties and had struggled for some years with his sexual desires towards members of his own sex. In his late teens he did not really know what to make of these feelings, and at times thought it was just part of his make-up. But as he got older and as his relationship with Jennifer got more serious, he knew that he was not attracted to her sexually and found their times of intimacy difficult.

He found sexual expression confusing, and it was only in his early twenties, after he had an unplanned homosexual encounter with a friend at college, that he began to think that he might be homosexual. It took some years of inner turmoil to accept this, and at the same time the pressure to conform was immense. All his friends at college were dating girls, and part of the identity of his peers lay in talking about girls and seeing who would end up going out with whom. Quite apart from this, the teaching he had at his church was that homosexuality was a perversion; it was morally wrong and God judged the homosexual severely, as it was abhorrent in his sight.

When he met Jennifer he liked her as a person, although he was not sexually attracted to her, but as he had not been out with a girl for over a year, he felt that to preserve his own sexual status with his friends, he needed to start dating her. And besides, he may have been wrong about his sexuality – he might find that this time it worked with a girl.

But it didn't work – in fact, it got worse. Not only was he unable to form any intimate bonds with her, but the inner struggle that he faced with his homosexual desires, being unable to express them in an open and social way, meant that he had sought for sexual experience with members of his own sex in places and ways that he would not normally have chosen. His sexual desires, because they were hidden and suppressed, were expressing themselves in lurid and impersonal ways.

It was only when Gary was beaten up by two men posing as homosexuals in a well-known public place for such encounters that he was forced to tell Jennifer about his inner struggle. The impact, as you can imagine, was devastating, not only on her but also on Gary.

Some of Gary's actions cannot be defended; he has to take responsibility for his actions, like we all do. But what he couldn't help was his homosexual desires, and what he also couldn't help was the attitude to homosexuality that he came across in his church and among his friends.

Perhaps if he had been part of a world that accepted him for who he was rather than forcing him to suppress his sexual desires and take on an identity that was not his own, he would not have been forced into the sexual underground. Perhaps if he had been shown the transforming power of acceptance into the Kingdom of God, Gary and Jennifer would not have had to go through such suffering and pain.

Social exclusion policy

By the exclusion policy that many churches have towards practising homosexuals, they have been forced to find identity and community in their own gay Christian communities. Whilst there may be benefits to this, there are also drawbacks. To force people into their own communities, away from the rest of the Church, and to isolate them means that we create a further moral and social difficulty. It not only damages the homosexuals, it damages the Church as well.

God's world is replete with paradox and difference; it is full of colours of every brightness and variety, of people of every kind and character, of sounds of every distinction. The Church itself is made up of sinful, needy people, just like the world is. All of us need transforming more and more into the likeness of Christ. A Church that does not seek to offer transformation to every section of society has no hope of changing the world.

Chapter 8

THE 'O' ZONE

Difference is for the sake of union and communion.

Leonardo Boff

The church-planting team were going into the heart of the urban challenge. It was an inner-city area that was over 80 per cent Asian and only had one or two churches. Most of the population were Muslim (although some of those were Muslims in a nominal sense), and there were a good number of mosques in the area. The team had no building, no money to speak of and felt called by God to work in this area to establish a witness for the Lord. It was going to be a long, hard struggle, there were no preconceived ideas about how they would do church meetings as such, and evangelism would all be by friendship and serving the local community. They would hold sports days for the young people, go into the schools to help the teachers, and have unemployment forums for those out of work. They would help them learn English; they had already built up a supply of food and clothes for those in great need; they even held fun days for the younger children, all at their own expense and all to serve and befriend the local community.

It was and is a fantastic vision, and commendation should be given to all those who grasp this challenge. Yet behind all these enterprising and indeed loving actions was the purpose of wanting to convert these people, who already had their own religion and beliefs. This chapter is about this whole area of how we relate to other faiths.

The 'O' no zone

The relationships between us and other faiths emerged as a considerable challenge in the latter part of the 20th Century. If we continue to ignore other faiths, we are not doing justice to the notion that Christianity is a universal faith whose message should be heard and lived out in front of as many people as possible. If we go all out to try to convert them, then we become guilty of a triumphalism and imperialism that puts us back in the position of the master rather than the servant.

However we feel at this point in time about other faiths, one thing is certain: adherents from other faiths form an integral and important part of our society; they are numerically significant and spiritually and religiously well organized and well defined. Non-Christian religion in Britain and the United States keeps on rising. There are now a considerable number of converts to all the major religions, and spirituality of all sorts is also soaring. Converts to Islam are particularly keen to affirm its values, as people try to make something out of the mess of Western culture. The opportunities for world-wide travel mean that people are becoming familiar with cultures other than their own, and many meet people from other cultures on a daily basis, whether that is at their local takeaway or in the more formal identity of their own religious building or presence. Such multi-culturalism is an acceptable part of life, and to many people the faiths that these other cultures bring with them are seen as viable religions, tolerated by some but endorsed by others.

In the evangelical Church, whilst we may have a real love for the people, we would be hard pushed to say that such an attitude of tolerance exists. Those from other faiths can all too often be seen as serving false gods, which are sometimes even personified as evil or of the devil. The religion is a deception and the adherents are lost and in need of salvation.

An issue that highlighted this to me recently was a discussion that arose with someone because an argument had erupted in their church which had caused quite a division. The church was one that was forward-thinking in its social action and evangelistic activity and, as part of the social action activities, those running the programme had allowed the church mini-bus to be used to take some elderly Asian women to the mosque each week, who would otherwise have found it difficult to get there. This had been found out by some of the church members and, indeed, some of its leaders, who were not aware of this development. There ensued a hue and cry about it: 'How could the church be using "the Lord's mini-bus" to take these women to this heathen place? How could the church actively encourage this service of a foreign god?' The church was divided over the issue and a bitter row was raging.

Yet if we continue to hold such views in a general national environment of acceptance, then we run the risk of being seen as less and less a part of the majority. If our distinctiveness as the body of Christ leads us to become isolationist in our views of other faiths, then we run the very real risk of losing credibility in people's eyes.

The 'O'utside zone

The reason why what the church-planting team did is open to question is that, however we understand what they are doing, what has to be recognized is that their action is more like a parachute drop than an attempt to build a bridge. For them, as for most Christians and especially us evangelicals, this action took place without first getting themselves onto speaking terms with those of the Islamic faith with regard to religious and salvation issues. We Christians have hardly begun to even open up the communication lines; they are still closed, and attempts at conversion without first establishing a well-thought-out frame of reference for mutual religious conversation will have little impact. It could even be said that it is rather naive of us to think that people who follow religions that are thousands of years old – some even older than Christianity – will change so rapidly after contact with us.

The action of going into a predominantly Muslim area with the aim of converting people without such strength of relationship speaks of the imperialistic approach mentioned earlier in Chapter 3. The reason that we are reluctant to do this, however, is that, more often than not, we think that there is nothing to discuss. They are wrong, we are right, and of course it is God's will that they should become Christians. We are automatically doing God's will in doing such evangelistic activity, because it is always necessarily the right thing to do – it is a *fait accompli*. There simply is nothing to discuss.

And the reason why the incident with the mini-bus causes us some disquiet is because we think that the mosque is a place where worship to a foreign god is going on; it is idolatrous at best, and evil at worst. To help this to happen in any way is to be complicit with an offence against truth.

Yet it is these attitudes that do not take seriously the scope and extent of the universal love and outreach of God which must be looked at if we are going to meaningfully engage with those of other faiths.

The awkwardness that we feel about these two issues is partly because there can be in the back of our minds a fear that thinks that we could possibly lose some ground to them. They are out to convert others, and so we are in danger of ourselves becoming targets of their missionary activity – or worse still, those who do not associate themselves with an organized religion could become their prey. They pose some kind of threat to us and our national and social fabric and identity. Furthermore, if they do succeed in seeing some converts, does this threaten our security in the God who is chiefly God of the Christian? Since other religions are trying to convert us to their faith, to show acceptance and emphasize mutuality is naive. They are out to convert us, so we may as well give it our best shot and try to convert them!

This attitude, however, is open to question at several levels. Firstly, whilst there are indeed people from other faiths who want to convert us, this is by no means always the case, and certainly my experience in inter-faith projects has been one of seeing an attitude of tremendous acceptance of others. This is also perhaps why dialogue is needed to break down barriers and suspicions. Could it be that the belief in Hinduism that one cannot become a Hindu unless you are born one, which in turn means that they do not try to convert people of other faiths, should be seen and heard more in this topic? They are far from exclusive and would encourage someone looking for salvation to work that out in their own religion. Is this something that dialogue itself would enable us and others to see and hear?

It is also open to question in that, if we try to convert others because they are trying to convert us, then we allow them to set the agenda. Our call as a prophetic Church is not to follow the errors of others but to be a lead to a new way of being. To try to convert merely as a defence tactic because others may try to convert us is reactionary and lacks vision. With regard to the possibility that we are under threat of losing some ground to them, come with me one Sunday morning not far from where I live, and see a church that stands alone in the middle of a distant field on the edge of a crumbling sea wall. Being nearly 1,500 years old, it looks more like a barn than a church, but it is in almost perfect condition. Walk through its doors with me and join in the prayers and the worship, which I know you will recognize, and I think this fear will go away. God is quite capable of finishing that which he started!

So, in the light of this, how can we see other faiths? What can we say about them from a Christian perspective that will mean that the walls of such suspicion can come down?

The 'O'uch zone

As I approached the Wailing Wall, my first reaction was one of awe and wonder. I had seen the photos many times. This wall of the Temple confines that Jesus himself had almost certainly walked around was an emotional and numinous experience. But my second reaction was to see the scores of Jewish people praying at the wall with an ardour and an urgency that was dynamic. There were thousands and thousands of pieces of paper placed in the wall with prayer requests on them. Prayers written out of people's pain, out of their love, their struggle, their desires, their hopes, their fears, their dreams, their nightmares. Was it really possible that God was deaf to these prayers because they were prayed by people who did not acknowledge Jesus as I did but followed only the God of the Old Testament? Did God answer any of these prayers? Did those who prayed them know him? Did he know them?

If we answer anything but a categorical 'No' to these questions, then we need to think further about our underlying assumptions towards those from other faiths.

It is not the purpose of this chapter to offer a theological treatise on other faiths as a response to God, but rather to offer some practical pointers as to how we need to relate to them from a perspective of evangelism. But to do this, a theological base is required.

The Bible zone

It has already been mentioned in Chapter 6 that we have in the Bible incidents where God was at work beyond the edges of our comfort zones. People who were not part of the community of faith were seen to be involved in the work of God and, indeed, knew God. If these people could know God, then that must mean that God is knowable to those who are outside of the covenant community of Israel, or the new covenant community established in and through Christ.

In the light of this, is it right that we Christians claim a monopoly on revelation? Are we the only ones to whom God speaks?

Jesus Christ is certainly the only name by which people can come to God, but that must, by definition, mean that in so far as anyone approaches God, that approach is only made possible by Christ. This must mean that coming to God is not limited by language, religion or culture, since the Christ who was crucified is the universal Christ who died for the whole of the human race (1 John 2:2). Their coming to God is made possible because of Christ. He is the One who has bridged the gulf, and though they may not acknowledge Christ in the same way that we do, this does not mean to say that they have placed themselves where they cannot enjoy the benefits of his life and death. Their openness to God may be a response to as much of God as their culture, education, experiences, traditions, existing beliefs and socialization allow them to express. To say that someone who does not acknowledge Jesus as we do cannot be redeemed is to place the cart before the horse. The very fact that they seek God is proof positive that they have come to a measure of faith made possible only by the merits of Christ, since Christ is God's way of salvation.

It has been well said that culture shades the human response to the voice of Christ. People's answer to the call of Christ can be limited, coloured, shaped and misshaped by their cultural and religious settings, yet this does not mean that it is totally obscured. Christ can be answered where he is not heard, known where he is not named, and believed on where he is not proclaimed. This was the basis on which the Old Testament saints were justified. Noah, Abraham, Moses and Rahab did not know it as clearly as we do, but their faith was in Christ. They were justified because of Christ, and they were able to walk with God because of Christ (Hebrews 11:13; cf. 1 Peter 1:10–11).

Whilst the Church as the body of Christ enjoys a unique relationship with the Lord, this does not mean to say that the Church is the exclusive channel of God's activity in the world or owns the Lord all to itself. A helpful illustration may be that of a man who can be in relationship with his mother, his sister and his wife. He loves all of them, he is in a living relationship with all of them, but the relationship that he has with his wife is the most tender, loving and intimate of all; he knows her on a level of personal involvement and oneness that is not true of the other relationships. So the Church may enjoy an intimacy with the Lord not known by the others, but that does not mean to say that the others are not in some kind of relationship with the Lord.

What is dialogue?

To dialogue with those from other faiths means that we engage them in conversation. It is the establishing of a rapport, of a harmonious relationship. It is a means whereby we, in effect, walk side by side. It is not coming to the conversation with a preconceived agenda of wanting to convert that person from their faith to ours; it is recognizing that all people are sought out by God to know him more and more. They are loved by him, and there may already exist a relationship between them and God. As messengers of the Christian faith, dialogue requires us to take our partners seriously in such a way that we both encounter each other under one Lord, who has given his gifts to all people and has woven truth into his world in many different styles, patterns, fabrics and colours.

Dialogue is not to be seen as something that is done for the purpose of winning an argument, proving a point or converting someone to our way of seeing things. We should not approach it thinking automatically that because they are of another faith they need to be converted or proved wrong. However difficult it is to accept, an attitude of mutual respect will need to allow for the possibility that it may be God's will for them to remain as they are in their faith, and that they might be more right about some things than we are.

Having talked this issue through with some evangelists and those working with other faiths, they often take it for granted that God wants that Muslim or that Jew or that Hindu to become a Christian. Yet this idea must be considered further if we are to establish dialogue. Whilst we should allow for this possibility and welcome it if it does happen, to come to the situation with a predetermined view that this is going to inevitably be the best thing for them does not do justice to the idea of difference being for the sake of communion. In dialogue we become genuinely open to the life-story and experiences of the other person. There is validity in their human story alone; their view of God and how they express their faith has value for what it is in itself. We do not seek in the first instance to convert them but to understand them and to empathize with them, and to learn from their experiences and expressions of faith.

In dialogue we must be prepared to become humanly and personally vulnerable so that in such an atmosphere of openness, both parties are exposed from within, and we open up in our relationship with God to a high degree and seek for the other to do the same. Progressive dialogue establishes openness and acceptance in a non-confrontational attitude where both parties know that the other does not carry a hidden agenda of wanting a conversion. Out of this soil we become discontented with the way things are; we are not content to leave without changing them or, indeed, being changed ourselves. We seek in the light of Christ to further this person's relationship with God, since we know and believe that Christ himself is present with us in love to draw the object of his love closer to himself.

In one such dialogue that I had, I was very open about my prayer life – the good times and the bad times, the times when I had been disillusioned with prayer and the times when I had encountered God afresh in prayer. Such an openness evoked a similar response from those from other faiths. For one person this meant acknowledging that some Christians probably have more of a personal relationship with God than some Jews; for the Jehovah's Witnesses this meant considering that the use of formulas in prayer was not the only way to pray (for them it is essential to pray in the names of Jehovah and Jesus). When this vulnerability becomes a mutual thing, and the listening to and the learning from each other is a two-way thing, then not just the others but we ourselves will be open to change. In this example it was the other who slightly adjusted their views, but in other cases it is me who has had to rethink some of my own prejudices.

Dialogue, properly conducted, is for the purpose of moving all the parties forward in faith. That those from other faiths may, through the dialogue, perceive contradictions in the way of life brought to the dialogue is a hoped-for possibility, but that we ourselves may through the dialogue also partake of new perspectives on the faith we brought to the dialogue is an equally hoped-for possibility.

For we must remain aware, not only that there is something true in other points of view, but that it is true by the work of the Holy Spirit. Christian truth is always greater than what we, in thinking, proclaiming, and indeed living, can capture. Dialogue requires that participants be open to the possibility that something else might be the case. That is, no matter how certain of or committed to their beliefs they may be, authentic dialogue is open to fuller perceptions of reality and new dimensions of truth. This means that in dialogue all are challenged. Christians too allow themselves to be questioned. Notwithstanding the fullness of God's revelation in Jesus Christ, the way that Christians sometimes understood and practiced their religion may be in need of purification.

Why dialogue?

In such an attitude of mutuality we become aware of what else can be achieved by a genuine openness to the other. It is almost as if the very act of talking to this person or group of people is itself an act of healing. The different faiths, instead of fighting and killing each other and running each other down, talk to each other with respect, giving space and dignity to the other. This can help to create a much-needed healing environment for our world. The differences that exist among us are there for the benefit of everyone, not to be compared and contrasted as in some puerile display of who is the greatest. The whole is greater than the sum of the parts; there is something in the connection made through the act of relating to those of other faiths that adds new possibilities to us all. There is something in the very act of us talking to each other precisely without the desire to 'win' them over, or 'notch up' another convert, or affirm our own 'rightness' by proving them wrong, that adds up to something greater than the component parts. Treating the different faiths as beliefs that can be marked 'right' or 'wrong' may not give us the total picture; it may be that the collage is completed only when we get together. To establish relatedness with those of other faiths expresses something close to the heart of God himself.

Hans Küng has said that there is 'no peace among the nations without peace among the religions. No peace among the religions without dialogue between the religions. No dialogue between the religions without the investigation of the foundations of the religions.' Religious discussion is an integral part of what it means to be part of a global humanity that acknowledges the interdependence and kinship of our common humanity, yet also acknowledges the need for diversity. If the whole world were to be the same, where would the difference be? Nothing denies the meaning of the variety of God's creation so much as sameness and the imposing of a single idea, a single conviction, a single way of living together, a single way of praying and speaking of God. Our Christian convictions are that the fullest light and clearest picture of God and his purposes come through the Christian faith. But part of living in this light means that we also acknowledge that God has given light for all. The true light has come into the world and shines on everyone (John 1:9), and perhaps sometimes others reflect certain things that otherwise we would not be able to see.

Salvation and dialogue

It may well be that readers have in their minds the question of a
person's standing before God when they die, and should they
continue to deny Christ, then no amount of dialogue will help
them. Yet it should be remembered that a person is judged by
their response of faith to the word of God, which is not always
tied in an exclusive sense to the acceptance of the gospel. The
word of God can come to people through their religious
systems, and we do not know what constitutes a response of
faith in each person's life. Their response of faith will be condi-
tioned by a multitude of factors shaped by their social, cultural
and religious background and experiences. The gospel tran-
scends all of these cultures, and that is part of what it means for
us to believe in the universal Christ whose lordship extends over
all the boundaries that we can construct.

Yet whilst the universal Christ can and does transcend
cultural and religious norms, people's response to him may not.
For some, their experience of the living Christ means that they are
enabled to embrace Christianity, but it will not always happen this
way. Their response of faith to the word of God may be expressed
within their own religious systems. Cornelius needed to hear the
word of God from Peter for his understanding to become complete, but for others no such opportunities presented themselves;
they expressed their faith within the framework in which the word
first came to them. So today people's expression of faith may not
always result in taking on all that Christianity is; it will vary from
situation to situation. Their response of faith may indeed be to
enter into dialogue with us! There are many people who only ever
hear a selfish, distorted, judgemental message of Christ or no
message at all. If we believe that they are rejected by God for not
responding to it, then this hardly leaves room for complacency;
ours may have been the greater complicity. God continues to
speak through the limitations of each person's knowledge, social-
ity, culture, religion, education and so forth, and their response of
faith to this word may well be enough to justify them.

The way forward for dialogue

There was a time in inter-faith dialogue when the tendency was to emphasize the oneness at the heart of all religions, the harmony of world community, and the need for consensus. Yet this approach has been shown to be inadequate, for a true harmony is one that comes with the recognition of difference and diversity. To talk of the oneness at the heart of religions is 'hypocrisy'; dialogue can only happen out of the differences in the faiths and out of the deeply held convictions of both sides that they have something that the other does not have. From this perspective, the objective is not to make religions similar, but to learn to work creatively and effectively with those differences.

Yet it must still be maintained that the purpose of dialogue remains evangelistic. Often inter-faith meetings can be little more than different religions getting together and being nice to each other. Certainly we should aim to be nice to each other, but this is not only what we should be aiming for in inter-faith dialogue. For the discussion to be progressive, we need to move beyond this cordiality and ensure that real differences are effectively addressed so that the discussion is progressive and we move the faith and indeed understanding of the other forward. Wanting dialogue to be a time when we try to share the revelation of God that we have in the face of Christ, and hope and pray that this will become a light and measure to the other people, does not mean to say that we want to convert them; it means that we continue to believe that what has been imparted to us in Christ is of universal value.

For example, at one inter-faith meeting that I went to, each faith talked for a few minutes on how their faith understood love. Whilst it was wonderful to see the areas of agreement, no one mentioned love as sacrificial – even the Jewish speaker missed this out. Yet for the Christian, this is foundational to love. The love of God is expressed through his own willingness to give of his own life so that he might redeem a fallen and sinful humanity. Love at its very highest expression is sacrificial.

So dialogue in this situation means that as Christians we can and should be a voice that brings clarity and furtherance to the understanding of other faiths. It will mean that we can learn from others; the weight of emphasis that they put on certain truths can be of great benefit to us. We can learn from other beliefs, but not in an entirely uncritical sense, for here too we expose weaknesses in their beliefs as we become subject to such comment ourselves.

We can perhaps learn from the understanding of meditation taught in Buddhism for personal growth and development. Perhaps there are some noble truths available to Buddhists in their path that leads to enlightenment. That the Buddha's only response to that which lies beyond human understanding is sometimes noble silence, is worthy of note. That which is incommunicable does not have any point of reference for worldlings with only mundane experiences and relative understanding to fully grasp it. Yet we can also 'argue' with such an approach, since the meditation and silence of the Buddha is featureless in that there is no personal being behind this ultimate reality. For us, whilst God cannot be completely understood and is in himself unknowable, he has chosen to reveal himself to us and is thus knowable. The infinite God, whilst remaining hidden even in his revelation, can be truly known, but only in part (1 Corinthians 13:12). When we encounter God, we encounter mystery, but meaning shines through mystery. We know God not as impersonal but as a personal being who can be loved and with whom people can enter into a dynamic relationship that is intimate and responsive. Such Christian insights need to be brought to bear on the Buddha's own insights.

We can also learn from the Hindu belief of the divine in every being. There is divinity in all of creation. All too often Christianity has located the divine in particular spheres to the exclusion of other ones. Yet to stress immanence to the detriment of transcendence does not do justice to God the Almighty who remains infinitely other, the One dwelling in unapproachable light (1 Timothy 6:16), whose immanence is an act of his freedom, not a quality of his being.

The 'O'nly zone

It is our willingness to approach dialogue with this mind-set that allows for other ways of engaging those from other faiths. If such dialogue causes some to embrace the Christian faith, as we hope and pray it will, then that is fantastic, but we do not do it solely for this reason. We do it to honour the God who calls us to share the good treasures he has given us with others, and to learn from the good treasures he has given to them. We also do it because in the power of connection there can be furtherance for the human spirit and the creation of a healing environment for our world, which all too often is torn by our differences rather than united because of them.

Chapter 9

BARBIE AND KEN

We refuse to bow to the spirit of the age, but we ought at least to speak the language of that age, and address it from the Cross in the tone of its all too familiar sorrow.

P. T. Forsyth

Late one night on the way home from the pub, Jim told me that he was having an affair. I was extremely surprised at the time, although, thinking back on our conversation that night and indeed other conversations, there were clues that he did not take some things too seriously. I always remember one occasion when he had tried to pair me off with a woman whom I knew was married. When I exclaimed, 'But she's married!', he just said that her partner had probably had affairs and it would even things up a bit. And that was pretty much all it was for Jim – it set the score even. His wife had had an affair and he was balancing things out a bit. He knew that if she got to know about it there would be 'hell to pay', because her affair was five years ago and they had worked hard at repairing things since then. So he kept it quiet, although he himself did not feel that guilty – or so he said – and felt better in himself for having evened things out, for having proved to himself at least, that he was still 'man enough' to have an affair.

When he went out with me he only drank a few pints (partly because he knew I couldn't and wouldn't even try to keep up with him!), but normally he would be on seven or eight pints every Friday and Saturday night, not to mention the mid-week visits after work. His drinking was because he was stressed and unhappy in his work, and he had recently tried some tarot readings to try to get some direction to his life. He was OK with me, but Jim was constantly putting on a front with most of the people I saw him relate to. This would range from assertiveness to sycophantic superficial niceties. I knew it was just a cover so that he did not have to really connect with people as he himself was, and in his more serious moments I got him to admit this. He didn't really see it as a problem, though, because this was how most of his other work colleagues were and most of his friends.

His relationship with Louise, his wife, was mundane. They would talk to each other non-stop about their daily activities – what they should buy from the supermarket, who was going to take the kids swimming in the morning – the sort of things that, at a cursory glance, would make you think that this was a happy and normal marriage. But they rarely, if ever, connected as people. Jim once told me that he did not really know what his wife's innermost fears were, what motivated her and what was unique about her that he had never met in anyone else. In short, Jim was lonely, depressed, disconnected from himself, without much internal or external direction – and really quite normal!

The story I have told is true – only the names have been changed. Jim and Louise really exist. They are really facing all these issues in their lives and they live in your street.

These two affairs took place because two essentially good and nice people did not really understand some foundational aspects of relationship and covenant, and because their lives lack some essential ingredients. In many people's lives there is a gaping need for them to not only connect with themselves and to their own inner spiritual identity, but to God, the source of all real personal identity and fulfilment. Experience tells us that many people's lives are running on empty, and they simply do not know where to begin, or sometimes that they do need to begin again to try to find out who they really are and what the purpose of their lives is.

It is this need within our society that makes the challenge to connect with people so decisive. It is this challenge that the readers of this book are urged to face.

'Life in plastic, it's fantastic'

The world and values of Barbie may seem very plastic compared to the ideals of the Church, but unless we really take seriously the fact that this is where their lives are at and attempt to empathize and understand their way of living and thinking, then we will fail to connect with them in a way they understand. Allusion has been made to the difficulty many people face when they do not take unfaithfulness that seriously, but for many others it is casual sex that is seen as perfectly normal and, indeed, is seen to enrich the quality of their lives. I recall listening to the conversations of some of the young people who were outside the church that I worked with, when they talked about this subject. It was plainly absurd to even think about marriage before having well and truly played the field, not only in committed relationships but in casual sexual encounters that would take place after a night out clubbing.

To them this plastic world is normal and to tell them otherwise is just out of place. They, their friends and their families have all lived plastic lives. But, of course, it's not plastic to them – only to me. To them I am the one who is plastic.

'Imagination, life is your creation'

Whether it is adultery, casual sex, smoking the occasional joint, or getting drunk, these are aspects of life that are still frowned on by the Church, but are seen as normal for many 'in the world'. We should not necessarily see each of these 'sins' as the same; they often have different causes and different consequences and are not all sinful in the same way. But what remains essential to evangelistic action is that it is not enough any more just to 'tolerate' these sins and assign ourselves to merely not passing judgement on them – an approach of acceptance without compliance, if you like. No, if we are to be really involved in Barbie and Ken moving closer to God, then we have to actually identify with why their lives are like this; we have to somehow get inside their lives. They are people made in God's image and capable of fantastic good, beauty and creativity (as well as great corruption!), who have chosen to live their lives in a particular way. We must realize that this is not the fringe – this is mainstream. We can't just dismiss them as the rebellious hedonists of society; they form a huge part of our society. Their lives and values must be allowed to shed their own light on our views and the type of relationships we build with them. To think about these issues merely in terms of right and wrong is to set the discussion in an inappropriate framework. A mutual relationship of respect will not be prepared to dismiss their values as corrupt. There needs to be a willingness to allow them space in a way that acknowledges that they too can live authentic and substantial existences.

Genuine identification with people will mean being committed to the people themselves and to the reasons why they live lives that seem to cut across the values that we like to think are the best and only way to live. These reasons should be taken seriously; they have something to tell us. Being 'committed' in this sense means that we have to be committed to the whole package that makes up their life. We cannot detach the 'sinful bits' from the whole person; these yearnings and the way they are expressed are part of this person's life. Being committed to them means that we acknowledge an underlying authenticity to their lives and even the 'sinful bits' that make up their lives – they too are part of authentic human existence. Their actions may have within them something that is redeemable, something that, whilst skewed, may have within it the seeds of a true humanity. In the case of casual sex, for example, it may be an expression of a real human need to connect with another. It is, after all, possible to express genuine desires in inappropriate ways. Commitment means that we do not see their actions as the 'bad bits' of an otherwise good life; they are intrinsically connected with who this person is in themselves, and may not always be as wrong as we often think. This does not mean, of course, that we should be committed, in the way the word is used here, to people who are violent, aggressive, abusive or dehumanizing in a way that society itself shuns, but in those areas which are the norms for 'the world' but not the norms for the Church.

We should realize that such actions in many cases have their roots in being part of a collective story. Behind these activities lies not only the deep human story of the individual, but also the collective human story of what has gone before. Their life, far from being an isolated isobar on a map of different-shaped contours, forms part of a societal trend. We should listen with respect, giving dignity to their story. They are part of society at large, or more appropriately, society at play.

However, being committed to the people and understanding the causes does not mean to say that we are not deeply concerned about the number of teenage pregnancies, the number of women who give birth outside of marriage, the number of young people who will have used some form of hard or soft drug by the age of 16. It does not mean to say that we trivialize sex in a way that robs it of being a rich expression of a loving, intimate and committed relationship. It does not mean that we are not extremely concerned about the lack of trust that exists between partners because of the history of infidelity that one or both of them has had to live with. Far from it – our concern and love for people is what wants the best for them. Yet our ideals have to be touched with reality. It is what we communicate to people and our ability to share with them in their experiences that are the issues that are pressing us here. Our ethical response should be one of engaging with the issues at all levels, but our evangelistic challenge is one of solidarity to people who accept such standards as the norm and indeed, have only ever known them as the norm. To communicate our disapproval only shows how far removed our values are from theirs. It also opens us up to denying the validity of the underlying reasons why such an activity is part of their lives.

Where do we begin?

Before we ask the question, 'What should people do?' we need to ask the question, 'What should people be?' Behind the question of the rights and wrongs of whether casual sex is OK, or whether adultery is OK, or whether premarital sex is OK, or whether getting drunk is OK, lies the prior question of what should people be. To get caught up with the question about *doing* before fully entering into the question of *being* does not do justice to the challenges we face in constructing an approach to evangelism that will cut the ice.

People make their life choices and live the lives they do out of who they are. It is this question that evangelism needs to be involved with, not only the establishing of certain criteria as a basis for what people should do.

Dig deep

In Chapter 1 reference was made to the story of Jesus' meeting with the woman at the well. It does seem reasonable from the rest of the account of the woman's activity in her own village that this encounter with Jesus was transformational for her whole life, and that in time her lifestyle did change to reflect the socio-ethical values of the day. Jesus' word of knowledge about her marital situation was not meant to condemn her activity, though – this would be out of character with the rest of the story. It was his way of saying, 'I know where you are and you can trust me.' We see this notion of 'commitment' here. There was obviously an underlying thirst in this woman's life that caused her to seek it in places and ways that were socially unacceptable and did violate something of the ideal of lifelong marital fidelity. It was only as Jesus respected this yearning and knew that it was in meeting him that such yearnings could be met, that this in turn would deal with these other aspects of her life.

All too often it is the imposition and expectation of rules that becomes the touchstone for relationship with God. How should people behave? What should they believe? What is right, what is wrong? But being committed to people provides its own dynamic of establishing relationship with them. It is in genuine encounter with Christ that people are changed into his likeness, not by the imposition of rules and regulations by an external third party. The relationship should come before the rules, and it is out of this dynamic that change should be expected. To be evangelistically effective we need to be able to identify with these needs where appropriate, and respect them as a legitimate part of the whole. Merely attempting to deal with the superficial symptoms hardly does justice to our call to proclaim a salvation that is to do with the whole person.

Transformation

As the believing community, we accept the authority of the Bible as that through which the revelation of God will come to us as to how morally and ethically we live our lives. Yet for moral or ethical principles to have authority *for* someone, this person needs to acknowledge them to be authoritative, since authority is essentially relational and needs to be owned by the person in submission to this authority. Authority proper needs to be acknowledged rather than mechanically or formally imposed. The real force and power of the Church's authority is part and parcel of it being experienced as true.

As those outside the Church do not have this experience, they will not necessarily recognize biblical authority in the way we do, so our task is to provide that experience for them. As people see and experience lives that do acknowledge the place for living by biblical standards of a covenant relationship, then it is the text of our lives that will speak clearest to them, not the quoting of biblical standards which only serve to alienate them further.

Often, however, the lives that Barbie and Ken live are due to social problems, not just individual ones, and here it is important that we recognize that each person has in part been shaped by society's values. The individual, whilst responsible for their actions, is also living out what it means to be a social creature, and to expect too much too soon may be unhelpful. For many of the problems we face socially there is a collective guilt. We, the Church, could have done more in the past. We could have been more involved with their lives. It is a guilt that we share.

Are you a member, Sir?

Katie and Kevin were both in their mid forties, they had both had previous marriages and both had teenage children from those marriages. They were both now single parents and both became Christians at about the same time as each other through the relationships that some members of our congregation had built with people at work. I baptized both of them and prayed with them to be filled with the Spirit. For a time everything, according to our standards, was great. They were regularly in church, contributed at Bible studies, became members, gave financially and Katie even prayed in tongues on occasions.

But two single Christians in the same age range, having had similar life experiences and coming to know God at roughly the same time, formed more than just a good friendship. At first it was a standard courtship, like any other. We respected this totally, and let them get on with it. Then, in time, they moved in together, and when they did, the church also got moving. It started off with the elders instructing me to visit them and talk to them about the biblical pattern of marriage. I was, of course, in full agreement and full of confidence. I not only had the backing of the elders, but also that of the denomination's hierarchy and, of course, that of the Bible, which made it plain that living together was sinful.

I got little response from my visit except the assurance that when the time was right they would get married, but due to some legal, practical and financial details still to be tied up from the separation and divorce, it was not going to happen in the foreseeable future.

Both continued to come to church and play an active role in the church's life, except that the church looked on and disapproved.

The second step was to visit another time, and this time to say that as a result of this continued living together, we would have to suspend their membership. They could, of course, still come to church, but not as members, since their lifestyle was not in accord with the biblical picture. I remember the air going icy cold as I used the words 'suspend your membership'. Katie and Kevin had possibly for the first time in their lives found a place where they could belong. They felt loved and welcomed, they felt as if God accepted them for all their faults, and here was I rejecting them because they were doing what all their friends and all their work colleagues and they themselves had considered normal all their lives. It did not matter that they could still come to church; the fact that there were now these conditions on their acceptance was enough to ruin it for them.

Both shortly stopped coming to church. It was a tragic loss!

About two years later, quite by chance, I bumped into Katie whilst out shopping. She told me that she had not been to any church since leaving ours and that her relationship with God was still strong, and that she still felt that she was accepted and loved by God.

You may dismiss this as the mistake of a zealous young pastor, but there are lots of Katies and Kevins out there who have gone to different churches and suffered the same or a similar fate.

What this does illustrate is that, had I been more committed to them as people and to this obvious need for love, identity and intimacy, then I would have been a lot less willing to separate the alleged immorality of the situation from its overall context.

Simply put, I failed to read the lives and values of two new Christians and had preferred codes of holiness over genuine holiness, which is about becoming a changed person through relationship with God, which, it has to be said, was happening profoundly in both their lives.

The reason that the notion of commitment is so important to our discussion is partly because the Church's very life is for the purpose of Katie and Kevin, Jim and Louise, Barbie and Ken! We are the Church at its best when we exist for our non-members. There are areas of the Church's life that are aimed at believers – those which strengthen, edify and build up – but even these are so that we might be better able to share our lives with those outside the Church in a stronger, more informed and loving way. Many churches update their singing, liven up their worship style, repackage their image, start to teach and practise spiritual gifts within the body of believers, give in-depth Bible studies and see tremendous growth of Christians from other churches, but fail to appreciate that all this energy and enthusiasm should be directed at engaging with Jim, Louise and Barbie, at helping them to feel that the church up the street is not the planet next door.

Start where they're at, not where we would like them to be

Katie and Kevin actually made it into the Church, but there are a lot who never do. They sense the disapproval of those Christians with whom they come into contact and what will happen to them if they join. They never enter the Church doors because the values of those inside keep them shut.

In the Introduction I suggested that there was something in the evangelical mind-set that almost enjoyed being negative about the world and rejoicing over the huge gap that exists between our values and theirs. In a recent survey quoted by a well-known evangelist in the UK, it said that of those people between the ages of 15 and 35, most could name no more than two of the Ten Commandments. This evangelist then went on to say that he was launching a major mission based on the Ten Commandments. It almost seems that if we can prove how far people are from our values, then this must be the place to start, as this is where they most badly need the help.

If most people are not that familiar with the Ten Commandments as religious propositions, then why start there? Why take as a starting-place for evangelism the very place that we have proven is not the most relevant thing in their lives? This approach does raise questions about what we think we are doing in a lot of our evangelistic efforts.

Black and white in a grey world

For Barbie and Ken, the evangelical world of right and wrong, black and white is alien to them in those areas that we think are clear-cut.

But in order to be able to identify and move with people, we ourselves need to become more flexible in the way we approach some of these subjects. We have focused on some sexual ethics, but there are other situations where we seem unable to cope with things that don't fit into our preconceived idea of 'acceptable' and 'not acceptable'.

An episode that illustrated to me how difficult we find it to think outside some fairly well-defined boundaries involved a conversation I had with some friends when the subject of body piercing came up following someone having their nose pierced. Someone in the group, who was not a Christian, said that they had recently read an article that said that piercing the body was similar to acupuncture and was thought by some to release energy channels within the body and to help towards wholeness. Also it was thought by some that the ear resembled the human foetus in the womb and whatever part of the ear was pierced affected this part of the body. I thought this sounded interesting and wanted to hear more from this person who was not a Christian. Yet within a few moments flat it was dismissed as 'dangerous' and 'New Agey'. It may well be this, but without the willingness to explore the topic or even to be prepared to have a conversation about it, we stand little hope of getting inside the issue or of seeing if there is anything in it that may be even partially true, but more dramatically of providing a basis from which we become committed to those who accept and practise such things. The non-Christian came away feeling alienated and that Christianity was not for him if it had such views on what he saw as pretty OK!

Sex, lies and stereotype

One of the reasons why we find it so hard to connect with Barbie and Ken is that we feel that unless we are 'different' from them, there will be no motivation for them to become like us. The desire to be separate from 'the world' has some very good reasons for it historically, and certainly as someone familiar with the Pentecostal movement, I know the sense of call that many had as they endeavoured to embrace a new way of living. In reacting against many of the stereotypes of the day which were seen as empty and hedonistic, Christians created their own values, beliefs and lifestyles. Some of the more mature Pentecostal people I know look back with a smile to the days when they thought that dance-halls and cinemas were the very places of iniquity.

Times change, but often the separatist mentality stays, finding different sets of 'don'ts' to regulate holiness.

But have we stressed our difference for long enough now? We know we are separate from the world; we have proved this beyond dispute. Perhaps now it is time to redress the balance and emphasize our sameness. Perhaps 'so different' should be changed to 'no different'. We can often stereotype people in the world as living in sin and without God, almost as if there is a stereotypical 'them and us' divide – a caricature that portrays those in the world as from a different planet, with whom we have little in common. Seeing ourselves as an elitist special group of people who are totally different from the rest of the world is argued for. Even our understanding of the Church emphasizes this: *ekklesia* means 'called out' – we are a called-out people, called to something better, something new. Whilst some scholars may suggest that *ekklesia* does not mean 'called out', but 'called together', it does highlight that, so long as we so focus on our separateness at the expense of our involvement, we fail to provide an adequate basis on which to be committed to the whole of people's lives.

To understand this we need look no further than God's own evangelistic effort, the Christmas story – which is not about God becoming a man, but about God becoming a baby! He did not come as a mighty warrior with superhuman powers; he had to come as a baby and experience all the growing up and hurts in life, like the rest of us do. Of course he was 'different', and this is also vital to the incarnation, but we must not lose sight of his 'sameness'. He had to become just like us – otherwise his work of salvation would have had no benefit to us whatsoever.

Redressing the balance and thinking in terms of 'sameness' does not mean that we minimize the reality of what God has done in our lives. We fully own our distinctives. If we are totally different, what we share is irrelevant. If we are totally the same, then we have nothing to share. We can share what God has done in our lives precisely because we are the same as everyone else; this is why we share it. What has worked for us is something that we want others to know about, because we are all the same. But it can only work for those who are like us, not those who are unlike us.

Yet all this needs to be placed within a progressive framework of making evangelism work. We need to think a bit more about how we do connect with Barbie and Ken, rather than just looking at why we don't connect with them at the moment.

Plastic's only skin deep

David's life was running on empty. He'd come into work on Monday morning and would start by running down his partner, whilst hardly ever giving a thought to improving his own life. He had little self-awareness or self-acceptance, he was quick to see the faults in others but failed to address his own. He drank his way through many of his social occasions, just watched TV most other evenings, and found it difficult to build lasting and solid friendships. He had been through one divorce and, the way things were going, was heading for another.

A great number of people in today's Western society, like David, live life on a fairly day-to-day, superficial level. Often this is as much a social dynamic as it is an individual's choice. For many, their world is made up of the everyday stuff of life – their families, their relationships, their social world, their enjoyment and fun times and so on. Whilst a life lived entirely on a superficial level may not bring satisfaction and fulfilment, for whatever reason, many live life at this level, and it may be through little fault of their own.

They are not in touch with the issues that make up their own life, never mind getting them to think through issues that speak about eternity, God, inner certainty, personal wholeness and the need for forgiveness.

To David the things that make up a typical evangelistic talk or message – like the life and death of Jesus, or the character of God, or the reality of sin and the need for repentance – are not things that he is particularly concerned about or has given much thought to. If we do evangelism from this perspective, then it will remain extremely difficult to connect with him. He is much more concerned about the everyday stuff that makes up his life – his children's education, or the health of his elderly parents, or the quality of his personal relationships, or even his own self-worth and value as a person.

But to get him to respond to evangelism, however we do it, does mean that he has got to go beyond the day-to-day stuff of his life and start to think about some of the more taxing aspects of life. Is there a personal Creator, and if there is, can he have a relationship with him? What will happen to him when he dies and will the wrong things he has done catch up with him?

Yet this does not mean to say that in the right context and in the security of a relationship David will not open up and explore these issues, which often lie dormant or just below the surface. I remember talking with a colleague at work, and I was telling her that I had just been to see the movie *Meet Joe Black*, which was about death becoming personified. She was someone who claimed no religious beliefs at all, but who was a good person and a good friend. She said, 'Well, whatever there is afterwards, it has got to be better than this, hasn't it?' Such comments are absolute gold-mines to evangelists, for they tell us so many things. They tell us that she has had her hurts and pains in this world, and that her understanding of life after death is a good one, but most important for my point here is that she had thought about life after death, but only at a superficial level. After that initial conversation I had several more, and the search for inner identity, conviction, meaning and redemption was taking place and developed considerably as we talked the issues through.

Education, education, education

So to get people to think about a personal relationship with a personal Creator God, we need to be involved in helping people to be more in touch with themselves and with their own inner identity, so that they will be better informed and more able to make decisions of greater import. Evangelism at this level can be about helping them through a whole range of different activities to become all that they can, to be more of the person whom God created them to be. It is out of what people are that they make their choices, not what they do, and it is when we have built relationships through our action and involvement in the stuff that makes up their lives that we can then help them to link this with spiritual identity and God.

On one occasion when I was in the sauna at my health club I got talking to one guy who had recently had a cancer scare. For him, as for most, this terrible and shocking experience has made him think about his life. He was jolted to realize afresh that life was brief, and getting stressed out at work was silly, and living to chase the pay-cheque at the end of each month was not what life was about. He said that the things he thought important before were not important now. His approach now was to value the simple things that he realized really mattered – to enjoy life and make the most of it with his family and loved ones, to try to improve the quality of his life. Of course, as I got to know him, I wanted him to start thinking about making his peace with God, about connecting spiritually, and to me this may seem a small step, but as I probed these issues gently, it was clear that for him and the millions like him, it is a gargantuan leap, not a small step. To him, if there is any life after death, it is a good and better place than the suffering he has known here. The question of making peace with God through Jesus is not even remotely connected to his current mind-set. To try to get someone thinking about the Christian questions at this level is still too big a jump. We need to listen to the issues that are live for them.

When we have listened to people and found out where they are coming from and shown them our love and unconditional acceptance and friendship, then they will be more likely in this context to think about some of the things that will help them to progress along their personal and spiritual road. Evangelism today works best at the non-verbal level through relationship building, and if a church lacks relationships with its community, it needs to find ways of building them, not as gospel fodder but as people worthy of our help just because they are precious to God and to us.

In this context, then, we can safely say that evangelism is about helping them to become more whole humans beings, about helping them to think through what it means to be them, what their life is about and what they will leave behind when they die. Apart from preaching a message based on salvation, it is about helping them with parenting skills, marriage skills, personal communication skills, health and fitness, economical living, drug abuse, wholesome sexual expression, financial management, career advice, rest and relaxation, the importance of reflection and stillness, education, domestic harmony, understanding your personality, family relationships, learning a foreign language, sensible drinking, unemployment, coping with guilt, coping with stress, ecological responsibility, personal identity and freedom – things which put them in touch with life, and help them to see that we, as Christians, are the ones who helped them to do it!

It has been well said that if you catch a fish for someone, you feed them for a day, but if you teach them how to fish, you feed them for life. In a framework of building our values into the relationships that we build with people, in an attitude of unconditional acceptance of the validity of this person's life as it is, with all its idiosyncrasies, we demonstrate the way of love, and if they remain outside the Church, then that's fine too.

But as they grow as people they will grow in their capacity to live authentic human lives, and one of the hallmarks of an authentic life is that you start to ask some of the authentic questions of existence – Where do I come from? Where am I going? What's it all about? When people ask these questions and are in a dynamic and vital relationship with those who have helped them to get there, we can feel that we have not only provided a fishing rod, but have taught them how to fish as well.

Perhaps then we can come in from the evangelism field and serve the master (Luke 17:8–10).

Chapter 10

TRY SOCIETY!

The point is not to break off the dialogue or to retire to the desert, but the word of God can be proclaimed only by someone who places himself outside 'the world', while staying at the very heart of the questioning that goes on within it.

Jacques Ellul

So far this book has addressed the evangelistic challenge from the angle of view-points and people groups as they currently are in our society, and how best we can engage with these from a Christian perspective. We have attempted to look at evangelism from a whole range of situations.

So, if we live in a post-Christian nation where people have become hardened to and dismissive of the word of the gospel, how can we best engage this from a positive perspective? Given that many people are on their own pilgrimage already, when our lives intercept theirs, how can we most profitably walk with them? If some people's morals do not appear to live up to Christian expectations, how can we both come to terms with this as well as become part of trying to build something better? Given that homosexuals experience prejudice, how can we become a beacon of light and hope to them whilst at the same time reflecting something of God's Kingdom to the world? – and so on, and so on.

But although we acknowledge and accept these facets of life in the modern world, we still believe that it is right to sit down with a blank sheet of paper and write our evangelistic agenda. But what will such an agenda, that takes seriously these 'givens', look like? We have addressed this in part through other chapters, but there are some more areas that deserve to be looked at if we are to go still further in looking at the evangelistic challenge for the 21st Century.

Evangelistic action

As evangelicals we believe in taking action, we believe that evangelism is something to be actively done rather than merely done in a passive state of 'being' or simply existing. The gospel, fully understood, means that we do have things to say, action to take, truth to impart and love to share. This is one of our hallmarks. How can we best do this, given the situation as it stands and given the fact that we are called to be proactive and proclamatory?

It is in this area where the evangelistic challenge takes on its most exciting and engaging form, for here we have to start to ask some more penetrating questions. For, rather than merely thinking of evangelism in the context of the mission of the Church, we can start to think of evangelism in the context of the mission of God. Rather than asking, 'What is the mission of the Church in the world?' we can ask, 'What is the mission of God for his world and what part can the Church play in this?'

When we ask this question, we begin to think more globally and more expansively. We can start to think about evangelism as something that can be done as part of a larger picture, that is the ongoing work of God in creation. Many modern-day Bible teachers have pointed out that the Genesis account of creation leads us into the ongoing creative activity of God, whose final work of creation will only be complete when all of creation reaches its fulfilment in Christ, and when the children of God are transformed into the likeness of Christ (Philippians 3:21; 2 Corinthians 3:18).

It is with this notion of God's ongoing creative activity in his world that we broach the subject of his ongoing purposes and mission. God himself still has a mission and purpose for the whole of his creation, not just for his Church. He has not rested from his work of perfecting that which he has made, but is still active in it and through it. If we believe, for example, that part of this ongoing mission is to help humanity to take greater care and responsibility for planet earth and its environment as a beautiful place to be enjoyed and shared with all people everywhere, and not to be treated simply as a warehouse of goods to be exploited at the expense of local indigenous people, then we will see that the Church can play an important part in this global mission by nailing its own beliefs to the mast and taking environmental action.

Identifying God's mission, and how it emerges as social trends in our own culture, thus becomes a key part of our own mission.

Try society

Similarly, if we believe that it is part of God's mission for his world to bring about a greater equality between the sexes and the races, then we will actively go about trying to do this, since such activity is profoundly evangelistic when done by those whose vision is always Christ-centred and Christ-focused.

If we see the mission of God as helping people to avoid excessive materialism and come to terms with themselves holistically, then we will be able to be involved in helping them do this outside the fairly restrictive agenda of a purely religious or doctrinal framework and concern.

To be able to think globally in terms of a mission that embraces the whole human story and God's ongoing creative activity in his world will become an essential part of taking hold of an evangelistic activity that shares the good news in those very areas that the good news itself speaks into. The good news itself is profound about issues such as equality (Galatians 3:28), the environment and the wonder of creation that has been given to humankind in shared responsibility with the Creator (Genesis 1:26–28), and the importance of living life holistically – the need for people to find themselves or come to their senses before they can be reunited with their heavenly Father (Luke 15:17). If the good news itself speaks profoundly into issues that can be engaged with outside of organized religion, then sharing the good news is sharing what the good news teaches us as Christians about these things.

The good news as God's word in Christ to his alienated people can be said in a thousand different ways. It can be said by telling the story of the Christ nailed to the cross to redeem all that is broken in our world; it can be said when we cry with the lost, displaced and marginalized; it can be said as we speak out for issues of human rights; it can be said as we accept those who know only brokenness and rejection.

Of course, our aim is always, finally and ultimately, to resolve the largest and most complex mission of all – the peaceful fellowship of the human soul with its Creator and Sustainer, God the Almighty. The path that each will tread towards such fellowship will vary greatly, and our job, where possible, is to help give shape to the voice of Christ as he speaks to women, men and children in the innermost depths of their lives.

Alternative medicine

Frank sat directly opposite me, right across the far side of the office. I didn't really talk to him much, except when he came over to use the fax machine near my desk. Generally, he would make some humorous or slightly off-colour remark.

But all this changed when, one afternoon, I got talking to him about the severe migraines he had been having. He had tried everything, but nothing had even come close to a cure, and he occasionally had to go home when they got severe. He said that he had thought of trying acupuncture but was not sure whether it was a lot of 'hocus-pocus' that would just end up draining him of money. I talked this issue through with him, since I had looked into acupuncture myself when I had a member of my congregation who was an acupuncturist, and I wanted to resolve in my own mind how it squared with Christian values. I told him as much as I knew about the principle on which acupuncture was meant to work, which led us further into a discussion and provided a basis for him to ask some more pointed questions. I said it was best to talk this through with the practitioner, but also that if we are to think of ourselves most fully, then we will appreciate that we are more than just a bunch of chemicals that can be treated with even more chemicals. We are living beings with a soul and a spirit, and because we often fail to see ourselves in this holistic light we see only a partial picture of who we are as people. He agreed with me, which surprised me, and said that he might give this acupuncturist a try.

He told me how the first treatment went and then, several weeks later, when he was still being treated and had not had another migraine, he shared more of his experiences. He had made a decision some years ago to try to build a more leisurely life rather than chasing around just to get a bigger pay cheque at the end of the month. When we talked about why it was that acupuncture seemed to be working whereas other treatments hadn't, we referred to our previous conversation and I said that many other forms of alternative medicine saw the human body as something to be treated holistically – that its life, energy flow and spirit are all part of its story. As I had his rapt attention, we moved on to the need to find ourselves and find a purpose for our lives that met our spiritual needs, but also that fulfilled a higher purpose than just a selfish one – to believe in a cause other than ourselves!

This conversation was left here, but weeks later, when I told Frank of my involvement with a church training programme – he was fascinated. I told him why I was involved in a church and why my faith was the most central part of my life. Frank was deeply moved – almost to tears – and certainly he displayed a sense of emotion that was a million miles away from the 'happy chappy' who used to make a few off-colour remarks by the fax machine!

The reason why Frank was so enthused by hearing about the Christian faith from my lips was because I had been part of something that was important to him – his health. At that point in time my faith was unknown, but when it became known to Frank he listened to it because I had listened to him and had been a part of him moving on to greater personal wholeness.

If part of God's mission for our times is to help people to realize that they are more than just material beings but whose spiritual make-up is profoundly a part of who they are, then we can see our mission as being part of this wider mission.

It was suggested in Chapter 9, 'Barbie and Ken', that often people need to find themselves before they can find God. This is not always the case, obviously, since many find God in their brokenness, but for a great many out there questions such as 'Is there a God and how can I relate to him?', 'Who made me so wonderfully complex and artistic?' and 'What is my purpose for living in this vast universe?' are ones that they ask only when they become more self-aware and connected with themselves. Certainly, the story of the ten lepers shows us that it is out of the experience of becoming whole, rather than just being cured, that the truest glory can be given to God (Luke 17:14–18).

If the evangelistic challenge needs to include in its agenda moving people on from a materialist view of human life, then our agenda could include ways in which we can be a part of this. This will be many and varied, and needs to work at both the individual and personal level, as it did with Frank, as well as at the level of the local church encouraging more open communication with those who are involved in holistic therapies.

As has been suggested in Chapter 4, 'Rethinking Revival', if revival is better understood as the Church finding itself in relation to those outside its walls rather than simply immersing itself in its own identity, then it is perhaps appropriate to think of evangelistic action as building relationships in those very areas that we identify as part of the mission of God. This will vary from person to person and church to church, depending on our own concerns, opportunities and knowledge. For the case in point, it could mean building relationships and creating arenas with the practitioners, patients and potential patients of alternative therapies, and somehow using this as a way to share our values with those we encounter. Alternative therapies are now an accepted part of life, with practitioners often being located in health clubs, recreation centres and high streets. Indeed, there are now some church leaders who are qualified in some of these therapies themselves. This holds open great possibilities.

Practitioners are often people who do not have a religious agenda to pursue but who can be very open to working with others who share some of their concerns. Of course, how all this is done will be crucial, but this is where the creative action of the Spirit is needed by the local church and local Christians, as they rely on God's action through his Spirit in Christ to provide ever new and creative ways in which to reapply and reconceive of his life and love to those who sit only in the shadows.

High society

As Christians we value all human life and are called to seek those things which improve the well-being of individuals and of society, and to protest against those things which detract from the dignity of people or wound them in any way. As those called to be a voice for justice, we should be prepared to speak up for those who are powerless, marginalized and broken, no matter what their sins may be. Being salt and light involves not only sharing the good things that we have been given, but also being a light in areas that are concealed and dark. Issues such as drug abuse and alcoholism impinge on issues of justice and personhood, and create huge barriers that prevent people from becoming all that they can become. We need to look at such issues honestly and without fear, for they strike at the very heart of what it means to pray 'Thy Kingdom come'.

Involvement and action in the social problem of drug and alcohol abuse can be done, therefore, in an effort to strive for a wholeness and quality of life for the individual and for society, which we believe to be part of the salvation and redemption that Jesus came to bring. Whatever action we decide to take, we can be certain that issues such as these can be tackled at a multitude of different levels. It may be, for example, that in the case of drug abuse we need to enter the political debate, or in the case of alcoholism we need to build links with other groups who work in this area. It is not sufficient to pretend that slogans or 'quick fixes' can ameliorate complex social situations. Rolling our sleeves up and thoroughly immersing ourselves in the issues as they stand is what is needed.

Education

The Church should aim, where it is appropriate and possible, to be at the cutting edge of education and support for a more creative lifestyle, and to be proactive in challenging the underlying causes of misuse and abuse of any kind. In the case of drug abuse, education should ideally begin before the likely age of experimentation – that is, in Primary school, where children are more likely than adolescents to heed the voices of those in authority. The Church could move for the more extensive use of School Chaplains in the realm of social education, and seek where possible to be involved in educating children and young people holistically. Education can and should extend to addressing the issue from the pulpit, developing pastoral care, building up the positive Christian values in young people and developing a holistic ministry that shows Christ-like love and concern. However, it should not stop there. The local church, functioning as a therapeutic community, will be called to live sacrificially and to labour without reward.

In other situations of abuse, ranging from the domestic to teenage crime, local workshops can be excellent ways of building local links. Lots of churches have succeeded here in getting hundreds of people through their doors each week to attend these activities.

The Church in action

Alternative therapies and the issues of drug and alcohol abuse are just two areas of society that are possible areas of action for Christians – there are many more. There are lots of committed Christians already working in these areas, and in a sense the areas of action that we decide are only part of the larger picture of taking our place within the larger scheme of God. It is not only the action that we take that is important, but also the attitude with which we do it. We must be prepared to seek a long-term vision for mission and to embrace a method of mission that is sacrificial and may yield little in terms of numerical or financial growth. This honours the God whom we believe has a larger purpose for his world than simply swelling church attendance.

This kind of vision for mission can become a voice that proclaims the good news from the rooftops (Luke 12:3), but also one that dares to speak to the powerful as well as for the powerless. It is not afraid to expose the dark deeds of oppression, but seeks also to utter things which bring a greater light. It speaks of the Christ as well as to the world he made. It strives for justice but not at the expense of mercy, for the divine but not at the expense of the human.

Imagine

When we are able to place our evangelistic agenda within such a vision, it means that we will have gained a capacity to look at things not only as they are at present but to imagine them as we would like them to be. It means that we will have let our imaginations run wild and will have asked ourselves what kind of a world God wants us to help to build. When we can see such a vision in our hearts, minds and spirits, it then becomes possible to walk with people in the wrong direction for the sake of arriving at a final destination. It becomes tolerable to be able to accept morals that we don't always agree with for the sake of sharing something that goes beyond doing and connects with being. It means that we can accept a faith that is misplaced, smouldering or hidden, because faith can always grow.

It means that we essentially see what we ourselves once were, but through the grace of God no longer are.

CONCLUSION

I felt as if I were walking with destiny, and all my past life had been
but a preparation for this hour.

Winston Churchill

As Job made his first few faltering steps away from his fresh
encounter with Yahweh, he was not the same man who had
stubbornly accused God of injustice. His persistent call that his
situation could only be solved with a word from God himself
was compounded by his invocation of God to plead his own case
against Job's accusations – indeed, he had made this appeal his
last word. Neither was he the same man as we meet at the beginning of the book – the unsullied but somewhat unenlightened
righteous man. For Job there was now an enlarged vision, a new
way of seeing. The God he had only heard of before, he had now
seen. He was caused to repent and acknowledge that he had
spoken of things he did not understand.

One of the qualities that Job had demonstrated in his
speeches, which the other characters had not, was his capacity to
respond in a different way to each of the challenges thrown
down to him by his friends and by the silence of God. It was
almost religion on the hoof. Each speech adopts a different way
of looking at his situation. By remaining spontaneous in his

responses and discovering an unorthodox way to emerge from each challenge with new and fresh questions, Job had demonstrated his capacity to think outside of the boundaries set for him by his friends. When he was finally shown things from a God's-eye view he was able to embrace a faith that was renewed, strengthened and more authentic. As he emerged from the whirlwind and the storm that had enveloped him, with the voice of God beckoning him to 'consider', he stepped out into a new understanding of himself and of his faith. As he saw with new eyes, all he could do was place his hand over his mouth and acknowledge his previous lack of understanding.

Just as Job was called by God to enter into ever new experiences and understandings of his God, so too is each believer. We are all called to take new steps of faith that involve leaving our comfort zones – whether that is by choice, or more often than not, being forced out of the safety of the nest we have known.

As this is true for each person, so it is true for each movement, each group, each denomination.

It is also true for the way that we evangelicals approach the task of evangelism.

To remain true to the distinctive of evangelical faith being one of personal encounter with the Lord and a passion for his ways, means that we need to continue to be open to what he calls us afresh to express and experience. We evangelicals have come through many tough challenges in years gone by, and doubtless will continue to face new ones.

This book has been about some of these challenges. Where we have become used to things the way they are, these may be the very areas that we are being called to transform with ever new insights, experiences and knowledge.

Yet the steps that Job made were no doubt tinged themselves with ambiguity. As we read the upbeat and positive conclusion to the story of Job, we forget that in many ways the problems were just about to begin. For Job, his fresh experience meant that things he had previously not had to deal with would now become challenges to him. What was his new doctrinal understanding on innocent suffering going to mean in his own community? The things that he had himself believed and taught, he now had to go back with cap in hand and say that he had got it wrong. How would he now manage more than double the resources he previously had? Such a growth rate in any modern company would herald managerial, administrative and logistical challenges that would stretch the very best to the limits. How would the rift that had occurred between him and his friends be healed? They had to swallow hard and allow Job to pray for them, after all they had said about him; and Job had to forgive them and not be bitter, after they had bruised and insulted him so.

Possibly the most significant challenge, though, would be how he handled the reaction of the community when he broke with all that was traditional for the time and gave his inheritance to his daughters! What abuse and derision would he face for doing such an outrageous thing? How would he respond to having his faith questioned yet again? How would his daughters cope with being beautiful, powerful and wealthy? What challenges would such a new way of existence bring to them?

The way forward for the evangelical community in its mission in a new millennium will likewise be full of challenges such as these – challenges that hit us in areas that are closest to our hearts.

But this is the only way of going forward; there is no other way. It is going to be a struggle but it is always worth it. The opening quotation in this Conclusion reminds us of that.

Those who would seek a new way of being must lay hold of the future with one hand and wipe the sweat from their brow with the other.

Christian Books

Timeless truths in shifting times

www.christian-publishing.com

News from a Christian perspective

Exclusive author interviews

Read extracts from the latest books

Share thoughts and faith

Complete list of signing events

Full catalogue & ordering

www.christian-publishing.com